TWAYNE'S WORLD AUTHORS SERIES

A Survey of the World's Literature

SPAIN

Janet W. Díaz, Texas Tech University

EDITOR

Luis Romero

TWAS 520

LUIS ROMERO

By LUIS GONZÁLEZ-DEL-VALLE
The University of Nebraska-Lincoln
and
BRADLEY A. SHAW
Kansas State University

TWAYNE PUBLISHERS
A DIVISION OF G. K. HALL & CO., BOSTON

Copyright © 1979 by G. K. Hall & Co.

Published in 1979 by Twayne Publishers,
A Division of G. K. Hall & Co.
All Rights Reserved

Printed on permanent/durable acid-free paper and bound
in the United States of America

First Printing

Frontispiece photo of Luis Romero by Toni Keller

Library of Congress Cataloging in Publication Data

Gonźalez del Valle, Luis.
Luis Romero.

(Twayne's world authors series ; TWAS 520 :
Spain)
Bibliography: p. 131-35
Includes index.
1. Romero, Luis—Criticism and interpretation.
I. Shaw, Bradley A., 1945-   joint author.
PQ6633.068Z69   863'.6'4   78-11449
ISBN 0-8057-6361-9

To
Luis William and Alexis Alicia González-del-Valle
Stacy Lynn and Evan Michael Shaw

Contents

About the Authors

Luis González-del-Valle was born in Santa Clara, Cuba, and came to the United States in 1961. In 1973 he became a U.S. citizen. After completing his undergraduate work at Wilmington College (University of North Carolina–Wilmington) in 1968, he studied at the University of Massachusetts at Amherst, where he received the M.A. in February 1972. In September of that same year he was awarded the Ph.D. under the Five College Cooperation Program conducted by Amherst College, Hampshire College, Mount Holyoke College, Smith College, and the University of Massachusetts at Amherst. He has taught at St. Hyacinth College and Seminary and Kansas State University. Presently he is an associate professor of Spanish at The University of Nebraska–Lincoln where he teaches courses on his specialty, twentieth-century Spanish literature.

Professor González-del-Valle is a coeditor of the *Journal of Spanish Studies: Twentieth Century*, *Studies in Twentieth Century Literature* and *A Semi-Annual Bibliography of Post-Civil War Spanish Fiction*, and editor of *Anales de la narrativa española contemporánea*. He is also director of the Society of Spanish and Spanish-American Studies. To date he has published five scholarly books which contain essays on Unamuno, Valle-Inclán, García Lorca, Asturias, García Márquez, Romero, Cela, Delibes, and Hernández, and two textbooks. His essays have appeared in numerous professional journals in the United States and abroad, including *Cuadernos Americanos*, *Archivum*, *Envíos*, *Sin Nombre*, *Romance Notes*, *Cuadernos Hispanoamericanos*, *Hispanófila*, *Hispania*, *Nueva Revista de Filología Hispánica*, *Chasqui*, *Papeles de Son Armadans*, *Books Abroad*, *Texto Crítico*, *Pacific Quarterly*.

Bradley Alan Shaw was born in Tremonton, Utah, in 1945. Having received his baccalaureate degree from Lewis and Clark College, he then earned his M.A. in Spanish at Northwestern University and his Ph.D. at the University of New Mexico. He taught Spanish language and Latin-American literature courses at Virginia Commonwealth University, and is now a member of the Department of Modern Languages at Kansas State University.

Professor Shaw is associate director of the (Kansas) Tri-University Center of Latin American Studies. He is assistant editor of the *Journal of Spanish Studies: Twentieth Century*, associate editor of *Studies in Twentieth Century Literature*, and consultant to the Society of Spanish and Spanish-American Studies. He has published *Latin-American Literature in English Translation: An Annotated Bibliography*, and is currently doing research on contemporary Latin-American fiction.

Preface

The objective of this book is to introduce to the English-speaking public the life and works of the distinguished Spanish novelist Luis Romero, a man who has participated actively in events that have dominated Spanish history since 1936. His works, as we shall discover, are in themselves useful tools for anyone wishing to understand the many problems Spaniards have faced during the past fifty years.

To date, no comprehensive book has appeared on Luis Romero in any language. Critical studies on his works fail to evaluate his complete production and to provide a cohesive view of his life. It is our hope to fill this vacuum. Our study is concerned primarily with Romero's novels. Most of his works are examined in chronological order. At times, however, books are grouped together because of common traits which reveal essential features of his literary output. Also considered are Romero's short stories, essays, and poetry; only his two novels and a few short stories written in Catalan have been excluded from our book in view of their relative unimportance in comparison with his Spanish writings and because they fail to add anything new and of significance to our understanding of Romero's art. Had his corpus in Catalan been more extensive, we would have treated this area at length. Throughout our analysis, we have attempted to shed light upon those themes and techniques appearing in Romero's literary production, to point to his development as a writer, and to evaluate Romero's talents and shortcomings. None of Romero's writings has been published in English; translations from the original Spanish are our own.

We would like to express our gratitude to Professors Robert L. Coon, Kathleen M. Glenn, and Janet W. Díaz for their help with the manuscript; to Professor Ignacio Soldevila-Durante for allowing us to use his interview with Romero; to Professor Antolín González-del-Valle for permitting us to utilize in our study some ideas developed in his discussions with Luis González-del-Valle; to Luis Romero for providing information concerning his life and works and for authorizing us to quote from the latter, and to our wives, Jeanne and Susan, for their patience with our academic undertakings. Also, we wish to thank the Bureau of General Research of Kansas State University for grants that contributed to the preparation of this book and Professor Ellyn M. Taylor for her assistance in locating materials through the Inter-Library Loan Department of Kansas State University's Farrell Library.

LUIS GONZÁLEZ-DEL-VALLE
BRADLEY A. SHAW

The University of Nebraska-Lincoln
Kansas State University

Chronology

recuerdos" ("The Treadmill of Memories") in the Barcelona weekly *Destino* (the series ends on July 11, 1964).

1965   Two essays are included in *Sobre la piel de toro (On the Bull's Hide)*.

1967   Publishes the historical work *Tres días de julio (Three Days in July)*.

1971   Continues his interest in history with *Desastre en Cartagena (Disaster in Cartagena)*.

1976   Becomes Honorary Fellow of the Society of Spanish and Spanish-American Studies. Publishes his most recent work on the Spanish Civil War, *El final de la guerra (The End of the War)*.

CHAPTER 1

Luis Romero: An Overview

I *The Man and His Works*

LUIS Romero Pérez was born in Barcelona on May 24, 1916, and spent his childhood and adolescence in that city's Santa María del Mar district, a typical and picturesque quarter dating back to medieval times. It is perhaps from living in this traditional environment that Romero developed his love for Barcelona.[1] The family, of modest means, had moved from Madrid to Barcelona prior to the birth of Luis. His father, Hipólito Romero de la Fuente, was a pioneer electrician in Barcelona. Due to the influence of his mother, Carmen Pérez Meriño, Romero developed an interest in literature. She used to sing ballads—"Delgadina", "Gerineldos"—for the children and encouraged a seamstress to tell Luis and his two brothers marvelous stories.[2]

From age eight to sixteen Romero received a traditionally Catholic education at the "Condal" school, an organization under the direction of the Brothers of Christian Doctrine. Afterwards he earned a degree in business.[3] During the first twenty years of his life, Romero read such diverse authors as Salgari, Verne, Dumas, Balzac, Cervantes, Valle-Inclán, Baroja, García Lorca, The Archpriest of Hita, Thomas Mann, Baudelaire, Freud, Dickens, Antonio Machado, Shakespeare, Dostoevsky, and Horace.[4] Romero did not follow any systematic reading plan either in his youth or later on in his life when he read such authors as Stendhal, Flaubert, Proust, Camus, Joyce, Faulkner, Kafka, Herman Hesse, Selma Lagerlöff, Conrad, Gabriel Miró, Azorín, Pirandello, and Borges.[5] In terms of literature, therefore, Romero is essentially a self-educated man. Although his readings were important in his intellectual development, he does not believe that they exerted a direct influence on his writings.[6] Also of significance in Romero's early life is his love for the sea, a feeling that he includes among

his first memories[7] and one that is still very important to him in his
adult life. From his relationship with the sea—by swimming and
sailing—Romero has derived inner peace and an ability to understand nature.[8]

Upon the outbreak of the Civil War in 1936, Romero, then
twenty, entered the devastating conflict which raged in Spain until
1939. He remained a soldier until age twenty-four,[9] enlisting after
the Civil War as a volunteer with the Spanish Blue Division
alongside the Germans on the Russian front.[10] This is the period of
Romero's life about which the least is known.[11] At times when
mentioning the Civil War, he has referred in broad terms to what
happened to him:

. . . We all had a bad time [during the Civil War]. . . . I was twenty years
old and I lived life with great intensity in one of the militant factions: July
18 specifically, perhaps I did not belong to a group, but I joined one a few
days later. . . . My personal adventure started on the frontier, in the
Pyrenees. . . , from there an adventure began that saw me twice
scheduled to be executed the following morning, that took me to underground fighting, then to the front. . ., I was in a concentration camp, I
was in jail. . . .[12]

After the war on the Russian front, Romero returned to Spain and
began to work for an insurance company.[13] As an insurance agent in
the 1940s Romero was exposed to the many social problems of
Spain.[14] During this period he traveled throughout his homeland,
meeting people of many different backgrounds and persuasions.[15]
The importance of his experiences during this time is emphasized by
Romero himself.

Much in my literary and ideological formation (in its realistic bent, of
course, and not in terms of stylistics), and my knowledge of Spanish reality
that would be reflected later on in my own novels, in my newspaper articles,
that is, my entire work as a writer, I was developing then.[16]

In 1948 Romero met Gloria Martinengo, who had returned to
Barcelona from Buenos Aires for a visit.[17] Romero departed for
Buenos Aires on December 31, 1950, to marry her,[18] there continuing his career in the insurance business with great success. It is
during this time that he wrote his first novel, *La noria* (*The
Treadmill*), a work for which he received the Eugenio Nadal Prize for
1951. News of the award was received by Romero a bit late, January

6, 1952.[19] The Nadal Prize was extremely important in Romero's career as a writer: it made him known in literary circles and encouraged him to leave the business world to become a full-time writer. The latter was possible with the 35,000 pesetas Romero received with the prize, a modest amount that allowed him to return to Spain with his wife[20] and to begin living from the income derived from his writings.[21]

Since the publication of *The Treadmill* in 1952 Luis Romero has written in Spanish six novels and two collections of short stories: *Carta de ayer* (*Letter from the Past*), *Las viejas voces* (*The Old Voices*), *Los otros* (*The Others*), *La noche buena* (*Christmas Eve*), *La corriente* (*The Current*), *El cacique* (*The Boss*), *Tudá,* and *Esas sombras del trasmundo* (*Shadows from Beyond*). He is the author of a few stories and two novels, *La finestra* (*The Window*) and *El carrer* (*The Street*), in Catalan.[22] In addition, he has written three historical works dealing with the Spanish Civil War—*Tres días de julio* (*Three Days in July*), *Desastre en Cartagena* (*Disaster in Cartagen*), *El final de la guerra* (*The End of the War*)—and a volume of poetry, *Cuerda Tensa* (*Tense Chord*), which he published at his own expense.[23] His first book, *Tense Chord,* reveals an intense love for life in contrast to the pervasiveness of death about him, and a concern for social justice, both of which become constants later on in his fiction.

Other writings by Luis Romero comprise five travel books, perhaps 500 essays,[24] an introduction to the life of the painter J. J. Tharrats, and a translation of Balzac's *César Biroteau* and *Eugenia Grandet*.[25] The travel books include *Tabernas* (*Taverns*) and *Libro de las tabernas de España* (*Book of Spain's Taverns*). In the former, Romero discusses those taverns he had known during his travels and proceeds to indicate his personal definition of what a tavern is. The book has fifteen chapters, each preceded by a brief statement concerning its content, a format reminiscent of Cervantes's *Don Quixote.* The *Book of Spain's Taverns* is very similar to its predecessor except that it contains a more detailed and extensive presentation of the subject. In twenty-two chapters Romero produces a history of the "tavern" as an institution, elaborates on types of wine, characterizes the typical bartender, and describes specific taverns throughout Spain. Each chapter, as with the previous book, is preceded by a brief note summarizing its content. Both books dwell on personal memories.

The remaining travel books are *Barcelona, Costa Brava,* and two chapters that Romero wrote for a book entitled *Sobre la piel de toro*

(*On the Bull's Hide*). The first two attempt to capture the spirit of the places identified by their titles, describing the histories and characteristics of these locations. The last work concerns Spain's development in the past few years (particularly that of its major cities), and speaks of the tourist industry in Spain (its growth, its positive and negative traits, what there is for tourists to do and see). All five travel books are accompanied by impressive photographs of Spain.

No one, not even the author himself, knows exactly how many essays he has written. These articles, dealing with painting,[26] personal recollections, travels, and current events, have appeared in many newspapers and periodicals (some of ephemeral existence).[27] Romero has collaborated with such newspapers as *Diario de Barcelona* (among the world's oldest), *La Vanguardia Española*, Madrid's *ABC*. Periodicals publishing his writings include Barcelona's *Solaridad Nacional, Destino, Correo Literario, Historia y Vida, Revista de Occidente, Q.P.,* and *Papeles de Son Armadans.*[28]

During his career as a writer Romero has received a number of distinctions. Besides the 1951 Nadal Prize, he was awarded in 1963 the Planeta Prize for *The Boss.* He has been named a Corresponding Member of the Hispanic Society of America[29] and in 1976 became an Honorary Fellow of the Society of Spanish and Spanish-American Studies. In recent years he has been less prolific and has sought refuge in nature from society's many pressures. Whenever his schedule permits, he enjoys brief excursions to his small house near the village of Víllec to contemplate the pastoral surroundings. Romero's concern with the basic aspects of life is not only an expression of his love for the cosmos; it reflects his discontent with society's oppressiveness toward man. To understand Romero's need to escape into nature is to comprehend the sorrow and loneliness expressed by the characters in his works: a highly sensitive and moral man, Luis Romero has had the misfortune to live in an amoral world.

II   *Romero's Reflections on the Novel*

To Luis Romero the novel is a reinvention of reality, "an invention based on observation."[30] It must reflect what is certain to occur in the environment the novelist has decided to depict.[31] In this context, the novelist works for the improvement of humanity as he presents to his readers injustices that prevail in the world, "the conflict that exists between man and society."[32] As a novelist, Romero proposes to awaken the consciousness of his readers concerning human relationships.[33] In writing a novel, according to Romero, the novelist focuses his lens on a limited space and proceeds to give to it such importance and intensity that the reader clearly perceives the problems that preoccupy the writer.[34] Romero is concerned with people, particularly with individuals,[35] as viewed by fellow man.[36] He feels that his characters should have independence from their creator,[37] and that, above all, they should be deeply human so that the reader may identify with them and their problems.[38] Thus a novel should present characters who, in their individuality, acquire generic traits before the reader, characteristics that speak of the common denominator of humanity.[39]

For Romero the artistic dimension of a novel consists in the writer's ability to employ the techniques that best express his thematic objectives.[40] Thus, techniques function as a means of deepening our understanding of the characters. As a result, each work requires the use of different techniques that will in each case capture the specific problems presented by the novelist through his personages.[41]

CHAPTER 2

A Poetic Expression of Themes

L UIS Romero's first book is *Cuerda Tensa* (*Tense Chord*), his only
contribution to the genre of poetry (Barcelona, 1950). The
poems are divided into five untitled sections, each one preceded by
an epigraph which aptly characterizes the mood or theme, and one
titled division, "Three Poems of Europe." At first introspective and
reflective, the poet seems to develop a greater awareness of his
humanity with each division of the collection. The thematic progres-
sion may be characterized in general terms according to the pattern
established by the epigraphs: (1) concern for the passage of time
(references to a popular song in which even the stream is not eternal);
(2) love of life and living in contrast to the loss of vitality because of age
or disillusionment (from the *Book of Good Love*); (3) joy of love and
spiritual communion (reference to the nude Venus, from Ovid's *Ars
Amandi*); (4) intensified passion and emphasis on physical love (from
an anguished love poem by Blas de Otero); (5) prayers dealing with
mortality and the desire to live forever (from I Corinthians, 3, in
which Saint Paul addresses the spiritually weak Corinthians); and (6)
"Three Poems of Europe," whose title suggests a preoccupation with
the fate of Europe, a concern that the poems present through the
poet's disillusionment with war and mankind's inability to achieve
social justice. What follows is a brief discussion of some of the most
representative poems in *Tense Chord*.

In "Yesterday in Today" ("Ayer en hoy", p. 13) Luis Romero is
expressing metaphorically the destructive powers of the past upon
man's present, and perhaps his future. The poem begins with a
question that allows us to comprehend the poet's attitude toward his
image in a mirror, which reflects in an objective fashion the deterioration of the human body resulting from the passing of time: "Should I
break that unfriendly mirror/or will I allow its coldness on my flesh?"
Through the images of "fog" and "land" we can visualize Romero's
view that the past as reflected by a mirror is simultaneously some-

thing ethereal ("fog"), pushed aside by man's present existence, and something concrete which remains with him, with his physical attributes ("my land"), forever: "This fog which is cleared by the living/ but fixed, to my land forever/ turns me from my failure and reduces me/ enslaves and urges me every day/ I do not know if to the past or toward the future." In this context, the past, something Romero is reminded of whenever he sees himself in a mirror, lacks substance before life and is, at the same time, a part of the poet that permits him to recollect his failures, perhaps propelling him to undertake new deeds or to attempt to relive what has occurred. In the third stanza the power of the past, its concreteness in the present, is further elaborated upon with a poetic and nostalgic reference to a house where smoke floats from room to room, carrying through its association with broken toys of childhood a reminder of the "perpetual truths" of the inevitable effect of time. Implicitly this smoke, the lingering past, becomes to each man an unavoidable and influential part of his present life. Thus, the importance of metaphors in the last stanza, "If my North Star does not point to the north and it fixes me eternally to the south. / How harsh is the travelled path/ dragging itself and yoked to those memories!" What the poet laments in these verses is a life ("the path") without new guidance ("north"), tied to memories ("south"). With "Yesterday in Today" Luis Romero is making a statement concerning man's existence, his morality, the constant battle between the past and the present in forging his future. As ethereal as it is unavoidable, the passage of time brings to all human beings a sense of their temporal limitations: if we are aware of the time spent—today's memories—which robs the future and enslaves us to our yesterdays, our perception of the cruel limitations of life will be enhanced most vividly.

"Spleen" ("Esplín") is another important poem in *Tense Chord* (p. 27). It expresses the emptiness of life, how man becomes disillusioned as everything appears to be against him. It is significant that in choosing a title for this poem, Luis Romero selected one in English, the language of a culture that to many Spaniards suggests the hopelessness of an "overcivilized" people. The word "spleen," as used in this poem, captures the idea of tedium and weariness. These two feelings become clear in the second stanza of the poem: "Useless to struggle and suicide/ useless the grace and power/ the wreaths of roses and even wine/ the afternoon prayer and nostalgia/ the promise of the sea and white dreams." In this view of the cosmos, it is pointless for man to attempt anything; his destiny is sealed. He cannot, for instance, expect relief in wine, for even though it gives warmth and solace, it dulls the senses and poisons the body.

Having read "Spleen," the reader is left with the understanding that man has to endure life with its many flaws. This position is intensified by Romero in another of his poems, one written in honor of the sixteenth-century Spanish painter Alonso Berruguete (p. 33). In this poem, Romero attempts to express the acute human suffering portrayed in works by the Spanish master. Human anguish results from being distant and separated from God, ". . . a God that being so high/ he escaped from pleasure. / A terrible God, beyond the world." What Romero perceives in Alonso Berruguete's figures is how hope has abandoned them because of the Almighty's inability to hear His creatures as they cry out in supplication.

The poems in untitled sections three and four are characterized by concomitant expressions of physical love and passion, and an almost desperate awareness of mortality. In "Contigo" ("With You," p. 49), for example, the poet concedes a quality of permanence to his loved one ("Fix me / in your smile / forever . . ./ Conserve me / in your closed hand"), but uses metaphors of sand and water to reveal a contrasting self-image: "¡Ay, I'm only / sand! / and clear water." He seeks stability from his lover, or in a temporal sense, a degree of protection from the inevitable effects of time: as he becomes sand and clear water, his hope of permanence is to be held tightly in her grasp. Within division four, the poet cannot divorce his thoughts from the harsh realities of human mortality, broken relationships, and distance or alienation from God. Not even the embrace of his lover in "Aquí" ("Here," pp. 71–72) is sufficient for him to forget the ". . . dead and buried boy / at the edge of immortal yearnings." "Superación" ("Overcoming," p. 73) pessimistically observes that the history of the loved ones is analogous to the constant and eternal action of ocean waves which roll in to the shore: their love is a constant struggle of continuing "highs" and "lows" from which there is no apparent escape, except, as the image of the waves which dissolve and expire also suggests, in death. "Orbita" ("Orbit," p. 75), however, does not reveal the anguished tone of the two previous poems. Instead, Romero is so moved by the joy and hope of love that he recalls images of renewal and life as conveyed in the "message" of delicate flowers and the freshness of springtime. But despite the desire to recover the "lost" childhood memory, the idealization and innocence of youth, the poet is still aware of the absence of God: ". . . and through the telescope of your life / through your amorous desire / I'll search for

God, the same Eternal God / whom I need so much and who unites us."

Total fulfillment is achieved at last in the all-consuming love expressed in "Plenitud" ("Plenitude," p. 77), the final poem of the fourth untitled section of *Tense Chord*. The absolute presence of his beloved is evident in the initial stanza of the poem: "I'm filled with you. I'm so filled / that not another image fits in my memory / No other body trembles in my arms / No other footsteps sound next to mine." Completing the expression of his obsessive love is his declaration that save for her image, that poet is blind to the rest of the world: ". . . I have no light or color / but your hair, your temples and your mouth / your profile, your waist and your word." The woman's spiritual (as opposed to physical) qualities are suggested by "your word," although the term may be understood to refer to her voice, thus evoking another sensual image. The "plenitude" of love reaches its ultimate expression in the third and final stanza. The poet surrenders his whole being, his life, into the "sure" hands of his beloved. In his mind she is completely and inevitably united with him: "And you've merged with me, unavoidably." As in the simple verses of "With You" (p. 49), the poet relies on the strength and certainty of the woman he loves.

The fulfillment of love and passion, however, offers only a brief respite from the anguish and disillusionment which characterize *Tense Chord*. Aside from the despair and frustration expressed in the "Three Poems of Europe," the most dramatic of Romero's poems are those which expand the poet's concept of both human mortality and the nature of God. These poems form the book's fifth section. "El Túnel" ("The Tunnel," p. 83) is, as its title suggests, a particularly dark poem of considerable gloom and anguish. Unlike previous poems, "The Tunnel" reveals Romero's longtime fear of eternal condemnation and punishment. He asks God either to lead him out of the tunnel, the anxiety of his existence, or take his life so that he will not suffer any longer.

"Herida de Dios" ("God's Wound," p. 85), the title of the following poem in the collection, is the constant and unshakable pain which God inflicts upon him. The "wound" is life, and although it bleeds openly, the poet asks that it never be healed (death): "This wound of God that lies open / I beg you, Lord, may it never close." The poet's yearning for eternal life is highlighted in the fifth section's final and most lengthy poem, "Eternidad concreta" ("Concrete Eternity," pp. 87–89). Another prayer-poem, "Concrete Eternity" is divided into

two parts: the first creates the image of his death and burial; in the
second part the poet repeats his claim to life and his plea to God that
he exist forever. The poem opens with the poet's reflection of death.
He celebrates skin, alive and young, and especially the blood that
carries life throughout his body: "I feel my blood, / between my legs, /
in my throat, in my wrists, / it sings an old song here in my temples"
(p. 87). The "old song" is the joyful noise of life, and perhaps, as
suggested by the adjective, a reference not only to his existence but to
the blood of generation after generation which links him to the past.
Romero's inquiry as to why mankind is "condemned" to die then
leads him to imagine the circumstances of his own death ("eyes that
do not see"; "a mouth which cannot utter a word," p. 87) and burial:

> To be earth, earth again,
> eyes filled with earth,
> hands touching earth,
> my mouth filled with earth,
> I don't want, I don't want so much earth! (p. 87)

Romero (he names himself in the poem) seeks almost frantically to
escape the path of the Grim Reaper, but ultimately, he acknowledges
the vanity of his actions: "I know that everything is useless. You want
me to die. / You send me again to the ground, without hearing me" (p.
88). The poet is totally alienated from a distant and hostile God. His
ruminations on death soon lead him to imagine his own demise, and,
employing the perspective of an observer, he narrates his death,
funeral, and faded memory:

> Luis Romero has died.
> Bells, the same as always, mourning,
> a cross over my name and poor fellow . . .
> He died such and such a day
> and on to something else. (p. 88)

In the second and final section of the poem Romero begs that he be
restored to life and that the "nightmare" end. The nightmare, which
specifically refers to his imagined death, is also the metaphorical

equivalent to life, or, rather, to the knowledge that human life must inevitably end.

As evidenced in the previous poems, probably the most pervasive motif in *Tense Chord* is that of extreme disenchantment. The poet has lost the innocence and freshness of his youth and any hope he might have nurtured. His joys are ephemeral, and he feels alienated and distant from the God of his childhood, the Baby Jesus who ruled with "his magic little hand" ("Infancia" ["Infancy"], p. 18) as if it were a wand. Romero's disillusionment is often associated with images of darkness, ashes, sand and earth, or physical separation (being "below"). Samson, who lost his legendary strength when his locks were shorn, symbolizes the poet's disenchantment ("Sansón" ["Samson"], p. 29). The "Three Poems of Europe" ("1941," "1945," and "1950") depart from the regular assonant rhymes of prior verses with more chaotic structure and imagery, reflective of the upheaval in Europe in 1941, 1945, and the aftermath of war in 1950. Europeans, Romero concludes, were like the Hebrews as they fled Egypt, except that theirs was a "Red Sea without the Promised Land" ("1950," p. 102).

As we have noticed, not all poems in *Tense Chord* are philosophical and gloomy. Some relief is achieved with those poems viewing love as a joyous event (for example "Amanece en Vilasar" ["Dawn in Vilasar"], "Retrato" ["Portrait], and, especially, "Posesión" ["Possession"]). The sensuality and transparency of a poem like "Possession" are representative of these and other poems from section three of the collection: "Flame, fix yourself here! / Fix your flesh in me. / Flesh, fix yourself here! / Fix your flame in me" (p. 65). With *Tense Chord*, Luis Romero revealed his great love for life in contrast to the effect of time upon man. The themes of social justice, love, physical destruction, death, and man's alienation are also very much present in this collection. All of them become constants later on in Romero's fiction. With his poetry, Luis Romero explores those existential dilemmas so important in his narrative.

CHAPTER 3

An Auspicious Beginning

*L*A *noria* (*The Treadmill*), winner of the coveted Eugenio Nadal Prize Competition in 1951, launched Luis Romero on a career completely devoted to letters, a luxury that few Spanish writers have been fortunate enough to enjoy.[1] The award, and the phenomenal subsequent success of the novel (the first edition was sold out in a matter of days), gained the immediate attention of critics and journalists.[2] Romero's popularity stemmed in part from the fact that his well-written novel was set in Barcelona, an added attraction to the reading public of that great city, eager to delve into what had been described as a kind of chronicle of life in the Spanish port.[3] Perhaps due to these reasons *The Treadmill* remains Luis Romero's best-known novel, both to the literary critic as well as the general public.[4]

The Treadmill is an account of contemporary urban reality, viewed within strict limitations of time (twenty-four hours) and place (Barcelona). However, the dimensions of the work are expanded by the creation of a collective protagonist; *The Treadmill* consists of thirty-seven short chapters, each of which presents an examination of a moment in the life of a new and distinct character. The author blends together men and women, young and old, professionals and vagrants, rich and poor, responsible and irresponsible in a seemingly complete panorama of society. People of all levels are united in that their individual problems and concerns reflect the basic and eternal human condition. A selection of some of Romero's personages reveals a conscious attempt on the part of the author to create a comprehensive vision of man in an urban setting. Dorita, a young prostitute, considers her earnings for the day and her plans for the immediate future. We then meet her taxi-driver, Manuel, who drives overtime to earn a few more *pesetas,* and who contemplates cheating the owner of his cab by lying about the price of gasoline.

A varied cast of characters follows. We see a student from a humble background who has studied conscientiously to pass the annual examination at the high school. An old woman makes sacrifices for her children, efforts which go completely unnoticed and unappreciated. A doctor who has a love affair with a beautiful and independent woman is ultimately little different from the lonely professor who collects books which serve him as companions in his solitude. A dutiful daughter contemplates her future in which, as wife, she must accept the shamefulness of sex in order to enjoy motherhood. Others who pass before the omniscient eye of the narrator are a young man who has begun a life of crime to escape the throes of poverty and oppression, an alcoholic, a gentleman with a certain lascivious bent, a gambler, and a widow who has inherited her husband's company and who now must struggle to remain at the top of a business world dominated by men.

Romero ends his novel with sympathetic and touching descriptions of an old woman and a priest. The woman remains unnamed, and little is known of her past except that she has reformed in the last three years after a life of sin for which she continues to carry feelings of guilt and remorse. The aging priest, Mosén Bruguera, offers her consolation and hope, and accepts her unconditionally as a child of God. Mosén Bruguera is characterized by an unfailing faith in God, a faith forged from knowledge of his own failings and weaknesses, which enables him to view with acute understanding and compassion the problems of his parishioners. The novel closes as the priest prepares for the first Mass of the new day, about twenty-four hours after Dorita returns home from a profitable evening.

Several critics have suggested that the real protagonist of the novel is Barcelona.[5] Such a statement is valid, but only partially so. It is true that the characters who appear to be isolated and self-sufficient in the novel are actually linked together in a human chain of circumstances and relationships, bound within the spatial limits of the Catalonian capital. But detailed description of Barcelona is less important than the portrayal of characters who might as easily be found in any large, cosmopolitan city: Madrid, Paris, New York, Buenos Aires, Rio, or many others. Thus the thirty-seven characters of *The Treadmill* represent Barcelona, and even Spain, but in an even wider sense may be seen to symbolize any urban society. In his first novel Romero paints a sobering yet sympathetic picture of man in his relationship with society.

I *Significance of the Title*

In *The Treadmill* a diverse body of themes—distinct and yet strongly interrelated—are brought to life. Primary among them is the unifying concept of the "noria," a chain pump by which water is drawn from a well in a series of buckets, and powered either automatically or by the more traditional use of horses or oxen.[6] Both the monotonous and seemingly endless movement of the buckets and of animals as they circle the apparatus have led to the figurative meaning of the term "treadmill" or "drudgery." Thus the metaphor of the title is clearly apparent. The buckets of the chain pump are readily associated with the characters of the novel. Both are individual entities—complete in themselves—which, according to their established place within the machine or in society, are locked into position and are unable to escape their boundaries. As far as the characters are concerned, their inability to free themselves from the forces which oppress them leads to a loss of communication, which in turn develops into a feeling of solitude and emptiness. Like the buckets of the chain pump which are dipped into the well, the many characters periodically submerge into the depths of life.

Another characteristic of the "noria" is the lack of meaningful change in its repetitious circular movement. Projecting this image to the novel, we find that the personages of *The Treadmill* display similar traits:[7] all experience frustration, suffering, and a desire to improve their particular status in life. These common elements link the many characters together as part of the human community. Romero depicts their lives as unfortunate, no more exciting than the endless task of the chain pump in extracting water from the well. Their labor is just as routine, their experiences representative of mankind in general, so that it seems they will be repeated *ad infinitum.* [8]

Thus the vital process of human existence is seen as essentially static, since its basic elements repeat themselves as life goes on. Exemplifying this concept is what is termed in *The Treadmill* the "hymn of the masses," or in other words, the hymn of the sameness of daily activities everywhere:

A healthy and invigorating sound is heard on the streets, music not perceived by the night watchers in this moment in which their defeat is consummated. This music, this civic orchestra, is discernible only to him who has just washed with fresh water. And, even more, it [the music] will only be heard by the initiated. It is different, subtle, and forms in its polyphony the hymn of the citizenry. All peoples, all cities have their corresponding hymn, and the countryside has, as well, its own music. The concert begins at dawn (pp. 11–12). [9]

Although the narrator refers in this passage to only one specific moment—the dawn—it may be said that all hours of the day contain within themselves a corresponding archetypal, absolute quality. [10]

II   *The Themes*

Having stated a number of the themes which are stressed in *The Treadmill*, it is imperative to consider them in more detail and to establish interrelationships between them. Throughout the novel society is perceived as an oppressive force. It is necessary to recognize, however, that this vision does not refer to a specific institution, not to political philosophies, not even to the oppression of one segment of the population (the rich, for example) over another. Romero deals instead with a kind of oppression which all of us inherit as our birthright. The following examples, in which two characters from very different socioeconomic circumstances find their lives manipulated by the world which surrounds them, serve to illustrate this theme:

She [Raquel] married very young; she was one of the most eligible women of the region and she had numerous admirers who felt, undoubtedly, defrauded in view of the speedy selection she made with the aid of her parents. She married, and of course is still married to, a very prestigious individual of considerable fortune, all of this befitting her own worthiness. She has not been happy in her marriage, even though this is known only to her close friends, or to the gossipers. Even if it is not very frequent, one can see husband and wife together and, of course, they are never separated in those places in which etiquette requires the opposite. In the Lyceum, next to his dress coat—one of the most elegant in the hall—her low-necked gown adds prestige to their box. In private life, however, things are different; their relations are more than cold, and the conjugal bed stopped being such four years ago. One cannot say that they hate nor that they despise each other, they are almost indifferent to each other, but there is no doubt that they need each other. The society which surrounds them has wrapped a rope around them which it is difficult to escape. She lives her life, within the bounds of what is proper, and he lives his within—and at times outside—those bounds. (pp. 114–15)

In view of his desire to work, he [Sardineta] went to the Unions and he was sent to the Employment Office. He wanted a position as a construction worker. Naturally, in order to work one had to belong to a union. He went to the Construction Union and was asked if he had worked in the trade, for without a permit they could not make him a union member. As it turned out, they were right, everyone knew more than he and convinced him immediately. In addition, everyone wore a tie and a collar and spoke so well that he, what could he possibly object to? (p. 218)

In the case of Raquel, she needs her husband in order to continue living, although unhappily, which is indeed a paradox. With the unemployed and unskilled "Sardineta" the oppression is different: his life has been reduced to the lowest poverty level without his being able to do anything to escape from the trap in which he finds himself.

The importance of society as an oppressive organization can be perceived in its effects on man. One result is the loneliness of the individual. This appears in many characters in *The Treadmill*, among them Arístides, Doña Clara, and Paco:

(—They fatigue me. Weariness. What does this fool know? What did he say about Angel Ferrant? Bah! . . . Shoemaker, to your shoes. Merchant stick to your lowly trade. . . . What is Roberto plotting? Is he going to hit me for a loan? Fatigue. Helplessness. Alone. My God! I am alone.) (pp. 76 and 77)

She [Clara] is proud of her work and is confident that her children, when they realize her enormous sacrifice, will be grateful to her. But, she is also sad. The children go after what they want, "mother" this, "mother" that, but she hardly sees them during the day and scarcely knows what they do, much less what they may think. Her business relations are just that: only business. "Madam" this and "madam" that. But the world of beings with whom she lives and struggles remains closed. With her girlfriends, it's almost the same; "Clarita" this and "Clarita" that, and once in a while a confidential word or two, or a bit of gossip; frequently a compliment. But she never has a heart-to-heart talk with any of them. She was married for twelve years and knows that between two individuals there can be integral, perfect, total communication, even without speaking much. She knows this well, and that is why, because she knows what it means to rely on another person, to understand him, to have no secrets, she feels somewhat lonely. (p. 153) (p. 153)

Hortensia seems very sure of herself and walks to the interior, turning on lights. The man [Paco] hurls himself toward the room he has been longing for. The sheets will be warm and she will continue scolding him for not having taken her to that refreshment stand on the Rambla de Cataluña . . . he will think of his savings and will answer with uninterested monosyllables. (p. 207)

In the passage concerning Arístides, he carries on a conversation with some friends and notices Roberto's excessive adulation of Planell. All of this fatigues him and eventually occasions intense despair and loneliness. Doña Clara, for her part, evaluates her existence and the superficiality of her relationships with other people, knowing she can confide in no one. Paco illustrates another aspect of loneliness: the impossibility of communication. On those rare occasions when he and his wife talk to one another, their minds are fixed on completely unrelated subjects. Paco is a person who escapes into himself, since everything that surrounds him is strange and remote.

As a logical result, the loneliness and isolation of the characters of *The Treadmill* provide as well a sense of emptiness in their lives. In the case of Jorge Mas this sensation is synthesized in two phrases: "He is not satisfied with his life. He would need something more authentic" (p. 128). A similar emptiness characterizes the life of Mercedes's son. Poverty, and the socioeconomic hierarchy which maintains it,[11] upset him to the point of contempt and rebellion (p. 142). Evasion of reality thus becomes a possible alternative to the anguish of solitude and rejection. Oppressed individuals such as the cuckold Esteban and the gambler Llorach seek a more attractive reality in alcohol, an escape from that which makes them suffer (pp. 227 and 261). Of profound significance, therefore, is the central theme of society's influence upon man. The novel portrays the circumstances in which the individual adapts and relates to society, effects caused by the influence of the cosmos on man, some of which, as we have noted, are occasionally perceived by the characters.[12]

Yet despite clear and direct criticism of social institutions and individuals who exploit others, Romero expresses a sympathetic, compassionate concern for man and his dual nature: the potential to be both victim and oppressor, saint and sinner. Unfortunately, even the strongest will is prone to weaknesses of the flesh and of the spirit. Luis Camps, for example, a man of many admirable qualities, lacks the courage to risk his professional livelihood by leaving his established medical practice to free himself and his mistress Raquel from the claws of a restrictive and unforgiving society (p. 111). Another example is that of Don Raimundo. His social grace and his wish to marry Clara are admirable indeed, but in moments of solitude the elderly gentleman is weakened by a desire for the flesh:

When this microbe [lust] attacks him, it's better not to talk about what happens for after all this gentleman, Don Raimundo, deserves maximum respect, because he comes from a leading family of the city, and also because he is a fine man. People talk in hushed voices about his "delights," and his friends, that is, the more depraved of them, make idle and off-color jokes about "when nature calls." (p. 161)

Raimundo's excesses are pardoned because he is a bachelor in a society which allows him a certain freedom according to the sexual double standard.

Others who suffer the ups and downs of the wheel of fortune (the *noria*) and whose weaknesses are intensified in moments of pressure are "Sardineta" (who becomes a thief), the drunkard Esteban (a cuckold), Montse (who surrenders to her sex drive), and Llorach (an incessant gambler). And even the old woman in the last pages of the novel and Mosén Bruguera are characterized by their constant struggle to do good in light of their awareness of past and present failures. The faith of the kindly priest refuses to yield to disheartening trends such as the attrition of workers from the fold of his parish. He prefers instead to praise the morning sunshine as a gift from God: "What a beautiful light shining upon the stones! Nothing is ugly, Lord, everything is beautiful, even these old houses are embellished by your merciful light. Every day my health is worse. It is a good hour" (p. 279). [13] For Mosén Bruguera life in itself is good and must be celebrated despite the problems of suffering and injustice.

Thus an aureole of hope, which is suggested in the final chapter of *The Treadmill* in the dawning of a new day, is somewhat confirmed in the ability to resist the temptation of evil as evinced in the examples of the woman and the priest, and yet tempered by the many cases in which man cannot escape being the victim of society and of his own frailties.

III   *The Structure*

To Luis Romero, literary techniques serve to enunciate "fundamental problems that affect relations among men."[14] And the novelist further states that "after I have conceived a novel, I begin writing it. In each case, I select that form of narrative that seems to me most efficient, most suitable for the expression of what I wish to say."[15] These statements contribute to our examination of the technical aspects of *The Treadmill,* for they justify our efforts to determine Romero's use of artistic devices in the expression of themes. Subdivision into thirty-seven chapters, each of which concentrates on a central character, provides a functional structure to *The Treadmill*. Unity is provided by having each character introduced, with more or less elaboration, in the previous chapter. In this way, the first chapter concentrates on the prostitute Dorita, while the second deals with the taxi-driver who took her home. In the example of the cabdriver, as with the majority of the parade of personages, the character who in one chapter is the almost exclusive object of the narrator's interest receives hardly any attention at all in the preceding unit. At other times, as in those chapters that deal with Clara (pp. 150–57) and Raimundo (pp. 158–63), the elaboration of a character is considerable in that chapter which anticipated his own.

Criticism has not been unanimous in the evaluation of *The Treadmill's* structure. There are many who believe this structure to be deficient, arguing that it is difficult to create a character in a few pages.[16] Our opinion, however, is closer to that of Pablo Gil Casado, who said that "*The Treadmill* tries, in essence, to give a panoramic view by means of a fragmented structure."[17] Indeed, if we turn our attention to the novel's themes, we shall see that the "panoramic" or generic view that these characters project agrees with what Romero tried to accomplish and actually did achieve. *The Treadmill* succeeds in giving a perspective of humanity by means of a multitude of characters whose human traits have become links that serve to solidify their brotherhood. Romero himself has expressed the opinion that an author must, at times, concentrate on something that exemplifies a wider scope:

> If a [magnifying] lens is applied to a portion of any writing or print, one will see how the space covered by this same lens will stand out and acquire an unexpected significance that is able to eclipse the print or writing.
> This is what a novel is, or at least, a certain type of novel, with respect to the total existence of humanity or a determined social group.[18]

Not only is the structure in chapters of *The Treadmill* effective because of its concentration (or lens focus) on a character, but also because each chapter, as it places emphasis on the individual and through its fragmentation of the whole, contains the thematic essence of the novel: we are isolated beings who are unable to break down and thus free ourselves from artificial barriers (social and structural so far as the unity of each chapter is concerned) which restrict us. It could be said that the links between chapters are weak. However, we must

remember that these same links, on a human level, are not strong in
the daily activities of the characters. They are "bucket-individuals,"
and as such become definite and distinct entities. The general
division into chapters contributes, without doubt, to the thematic
objectives of *The Treadmill.*

Aside from what we have mentioned of the structure of the work,
there remains another important aspect to be discussed. *The Treadmill* offers a day in the life of a group of people.[19] When Romero
selected this period of time, he conceived it as representative of a
cycle that is manageable for the novelist due to its limitations and
because it allows him to say implicitly "behold a day among many in
the lives of a few persons." In this way, there is a ratification of the
view of repetition that both the title and the objectives of the novel
project to the reader. The work's first paragraph testifies to the fact
that there is no doubt but that in *The Treadmill* the narrator is trying
to provide a view of daily life:

> Dawn breaks. No one knows exactly when this fragile brightness emerged
> above the rooftops of the city. A new and unknown sound vibrates in the air,
> and in the atmosphere the daily miracle is taking place. (p. 9)

The coming of dawn, as in this passage, is symbolic of the recurrent
cycle of life in the city.[20]

While considering the structure of *The Treadmill,* one must add
that there are many small details by which its author gives unity to the
novel without detracting from the fragmentary effect that functions to
underscore the themes of alienation and the lack of communication in
modern urban society. Three techniques are particularly important.
First, there is a tendency to give a greater temporal density to what is
narrated, by presenting multiple events that transpire at a given
moment. For example, when Alicia eats lunch with her parents the
reader sees simultaneous actions:

> The father, with his mouth full, continues without anyone listening;
> —Some representatives from the Treasury Department came; I realized it
> at once and ordered Puig to . . .
> (—This afternoon at "The Farmhouse." Good atmosphere. Dance a little.
> Ignacio, handsome, strong, tanned. Get married? Hummm! Can't be sure.
> Thirty-seven years old; a bad age. Hard to break. Engineer; handsome. Let
> 'em eat their hearts out! Property dad.)
> The youngest has spilled a glass of water on the tablecloth; an embroidered

one which, if they were not so rich, would be reserved only for Sundays. (p. 61)[21]

It is implicit in this passage that even though Alicia's reality is of primary interst, there are other "realities" occurring simultaneously with hers. The attempt to give a wider view of life does not manifest itself solely within the limited framework of each individual chapter. Often, events that occur at the same time are given in different chapters (for instance, Alvaro's arrival at the bookstore on pages 29 and 31).

Second, Romero offers a double perspective, as when Lola and Alvaro evaluate each other:

(—It must be a novel. Valbuena? Valbuena? He watches me a lot; now he's looking at my legs. . . . Now he's going to browse through the books on the shelves. What a screwball! Always asking about rare books. I don't know why he would want those old things). (p. 30)
(—Anyhow I'm not going to buy it . . . no; they said four hundred or so, but I'll check on the exact price just in case. . . . I could also sell the old volume and pay the difference. Rogelio's not here; I'll ask the girl. What legs! Stupid; almost completely so . . . she doesn't have the slightest idea about what I'm asking her. She probably thinks it's a cookbook or some other silly thing). (p. 31)[22]

There are two results of this double perspective: a chronological link is established between two characters, because both are thinking at the same time, and we have a reaffirmation of the belief that man is an island, due in part to the fact that he sees things from his private and uniuqe viewpoint.

Lastly, the unity of the novel is maintained by means of references to secondary events that repeat themselves as a result of the fact that all characters reside in the same city. In the first chapter Juanchu gives to Dorita a bouquet of carnations. These carnations were just cut and still "have drops of dew from the fields" (p. 10). Almost at the end of the novel, at dawn the following day, there is again a reference to flowers: "The first cart of flowers has arrived at the Rambla, a small, light cart pulled by an early-rising pony. The flowers come moist and fragrant to perfume the city, to redeem it" (p. 263). The moistness of the flowers during the yesterday and today of the novel ratifies the cyclical process of events. Another detail that also repeats itself and that, as such, gives unity, is the reference made to a speech given by

the Minister of Public Works, a document printed on the front page of
a newspaper (pp. 19 and 42).

IV *Narrative Techniques*

Of great importance in our study of literary devices are the narrative
techniques used in *The Treadmill*. On this aspect a few critics have
expressed themselves negatively.[23] None of them, however, has
offered an analysis of these techniques and their objectives. In *The
Treadmill* we find interior monologues, stream of consciousness,
descriptions and comments by the narrator, and dialogues. The
interior monologues are of two kinds: indirect and direct.[24] Examples
of the indirect interior monologue are very common: "At the back of
her neck, under her hair, his sleeve is tickling her. Ten hours earlier
they didn't even know each other. but she's used to squeezing
friendship as if it were a lemon, until no juice is left" (p. 9). In this
quote, Dorita is heard, in third person, thinking about Juanchu. At
the same time, one can detect the presence of a narrator directing the
reader as he says "she is used to squeezing friendship as if it were a
lemon, until no juice is left."[25]

What complicates this technique is that at times the narrator does
not limit himself to guiding us through the thoughts of a character like
Dorita. Often, he offers his own comments, as when he speaks of
things Dorita has not seen:

Along the Ronda go the squeaking trolley cars, like red streamers
announcing dawn in the city. And now, if Dorita were to notice such things,
she would see the loveliest palm trees of the whole area: those which sway
gracefully in the plaza of the university. (p. 11)

This neighborhood has undergone a great transformation although Dorita
may be unaware of it, because she arrived from the country just five years
ago. (p. 12)

In the two passages, the narrator is omniscient; he knows what she
has and has not thought. However, the presence of the narrator, as he
adds to what takes place, does not diminish the effectiveness of the
novel. *The Treadmill* only suffers insofar as the comments of the
narrator are concerned, when these statements lose their objectivity.

Typical of the manner in which the narrator expresses his viewpoints by blending them into the narrative is his description of the
homosexual Arístades: "In this man's life there is a secret which some

know and others suspect (I do not speak of those who share it)" (p. 74). This parenthetical observation on the homosexuals with whom Arístides associates, although providing irony, is not needed in the novel and reflects the displeasure of the narrator toward something that he dislikes (in this case, homosexuality). The effect of the imposition of the narrator's morality on the work is often negative because the characters lose their liberty as the distance between the creator and his creations is destroyed. An example of the self-defeating intervention of the narrator is perceived with Carlos Pi. In this case, it is not necessary for the narrator to interpret this character for us, and what is more important, it would be better if Carlos Pi were to come to life before the reader without obvious assistance from anyone:

> The Publi Theater is the refuge of those who need to kill about an hour's time; it is also good for the person who must forget a problem for the same length of time. Among the latter is Carlos Pi, a man blessed by fortune and envied by all who know him. (p. 104)[26]

It should be pointed out, however, that comments and descriptions by the omniscient narrator function, at times, in the articulation of the theme of human duality in the novel. By presenting situations in which only the omniscient narrator's point of view is given, a pattern soon develops in which the author either rejects on moral or ethical grounds the actions of individuals or institutions, or sympathetically and compassionately accepts their shortcomings. Such a dichotomization allows for a rather stern ethical vision of man and society, expressed with equally strong recognition of the continual frustrations of life, its temptations and imperfections.

Criticism of society and its institutions by the omniscient narrator is direct and uncompromising, and is often presented behind a transparent veil of irony. For example, the Insurance Company is said to offer benefits to employees which "never go beyond the theoretical" (p. 88), and usurers are justified in their noble and "meritorious" practice of lending money.[27] On another occasion the narrator briefly suspends his objectivity in order to attack the self-satisfaction and indifference of the middle class:

> The city is dining; that is, this middle-class sector of the city. Workers and artisans must already be in bed; the others, no one ever knows when they eat, nor if they even do, nor when they finally retire for the night. (p. 163)

This tongue-in-cheek attitude is typical of other passages in the novel
where Romero wishes to criticize a social convention or tradition.

The narrator's attitude toward some characters, however, is much
less severe. The censure of Arístides ("perverted body," p. 76),
Carlos Pi ("blessed by fortune," p. 104), and Llorach ("he's made a
mistake, and what is still more regrettable is that he gained nothing at
all from it," p. 258) is tempered by equal recognition that they are
victims of themselves and of society.[28] The tendency to accept the
failings of his characters is clearly evident in the case of Raimundo,[29]
Trini (she is, after all, discreet in keeping confidential her sexual
relations with government and business leaders), and the unhappily
married Hortensia and Paco:

If Hortensia had married another man, surely it wouldn't be this way. One
shouldn't place all the blame on her, although it would be unjust to accuse
Paco of his wife's always unsatisfied flirting. Things are just as they are. (p.
200)

Both parties are forgiven for a situation which undoubtedly has many
causes.

In fact, the narrator shows greatest understanding not because of
the characters' ability to succeed, but because of the degree to which
they have had to struggle in their efforts to live a decent and dignified
life. Roberto has fought his way from a background of poverty to a
position in which he plans to escape from the sterilizing effect of the
city into the interior of Brazil, where he hopes to find meaning and
fulfillment, "where risk and discomfort have their reward, where his
heart may unite with others, where, honoring his lineage, he again
may be able to serve mankind" (p. 81). It is not surprising, either, that
the priest and the old woman at the end of the novel are sympathetically portrayed for having persisted in their struggle for self-respect.

For these characters, and others, the omniscient narrator concedes
that God is the ultimate judge of one's actions and intentions. The
concept of God in the novel is first introduced from the point of view
of the guilt-ridden Trini. She refuses to enter a church because she
feels rejected by God:

The place where she has never dared to set foot is the church. She doesn't
think that the priest would say anything, but God surely can't view her very
favorably, and God is always in her hometown church, perhaps only there.
(p. 170)

This concept is further developed in the case of the old woman. Although she does not attend church, she is preoccupied with the idea of dying without a proper burial ("as God so commands" [naturally], and is heartened by the assurance of Mosén Bruguera that God accepts her as she is.

Finally, in describing the thoughts of the priest, the narrator elucidates the theme of man's dual nature:

> But God reads our hearts and minds and knows everything that we think and want, knows all our faults, and knows when the spirit yields, even if for only a few seconds, to temptation. If Satan were only that monster of horns and trident, how easy it would be to fight him! But there is a Satan deep within each of us who constantly spies on us and gives our weary souls no rest, and [therefore] they must be always on guard if they do not wish to perish. (pp. 276–77)
>
> . . . Everything conspires against Man, and only God's forgiveness can save him. (p. 277)

Man's potential for both good and evil is ever present, and he must constantly try to conquer the "devil" within him. Unfortunately, much of the poignancy of this description of the "human condition" is weakened by the didactic intrusion of the narrator into the lives of the characters. Nonetheless, it remains an important factor in the novel, revealing the narrator's strong discontent with social institutions and his concern for the quality of human existence.

It must be added that the presence of the narrator (or author) in *The Treadmill* is a significant phenomenon, if one keeps in mind some comments made by Romero:

> The author cannot accept responsibility for the way his characters see things: he must allow them to be free. The responsibility that the author accepts completely is that of the novel.[30] . . . I have allowed my characters to express themselves with freedom, and only once in a while—such are the defects or privileges of the trade—the opinion of the novelist appears blended with those of the character or he slips in a comment almost by accident.[31]

These remarks, made after *The Treadmill* was published, reveal a certain confusion on the part of the novelist. In the first passage, he speaks of the freedom of the characters, while in the second, he cannot distinguish as to whether the presence of the narrator weakens or contributes positively to a novel.

Direct interior monologues are not common in *The Treadmill*.[32] They appear assimilated into the indirect interior monologues:

The conversation lasts ten minutes or more, since women are so fond of chatting on the phone. Ignacio surely was in a hurry; he was [still] soaked [from his swim] when he spoke from the Club's telephone booth; someone was waiting and, nevertheless, there wasn't a way to end the conversation. Besides Alicia, she's so beautiful! I said beautiful, not cute. I said beautiful, not intelligent. I said beautiful, but not good; although I don't think she's bad either. (pp. 58–59)

The change in perspective from third to first person gives greater intimacy to the thoughts of Ignacio, this intimacy being a desirable objective because the character is thinking of his fiancée.

Romero's use of stream of consciousness is only partially successful in revealing the inner thoughts of each protagonist.[33] We are referring to those passages in the first person that are typographically marked in the novel, appearing within parentheses. While calling this technique stream of consciousness, we do so in awareness of Romero's failure to develop fully the potential of the technique. These passages seem to be in a period of gestation; they are not as effective as they should be, due in part to their brevity. From this shortness emanates a fundamental defect: in the direct exposition of the mental processes, these paragraphs are somewhat weak. Also, the fact that they are dispersed among interior monologues indicates a degree of selectivity that in turn diminishes the authenticity that must characterize the stream of consciousness. If we have characters giving their thoughts directly at a prespeech level, how is it possible for the perspective to change from stream of consciousness (where no narrator is involved) to interior monologue (where there is authorial intervention)?

However, the following example will point out how, in most instances, these passages show the characteristics of stream of consciousness:

(—How "chic"! Good orchestra. Soft hand, light tobacco. "Don't trust, don't trust." Broad shoulders, light tobacco; like in the movies . . . so happy. I don't care. Well, who knows? "Don't trust . . . don't trust." But . . . I liked him so much! Pretty; tailored suit, sheer nylons. His hand so tender . . . led me with confidence. Then . . . well, then . . .! "Oh, Mr. Colón. —Oh, Mr. Colón! — Look how the world is. —Oh, Mr. Colón. . . .!" Madness. Foolishness. "Don't go to El Rigat [a night club] . . . it's not to be trusted."

Envy. My Sunday, mine, mine. Love. I do what I want to do; nothing else matters. Let them just try to take away from me what's done ["what is danced"]). (pp. 27–28)

Lola's ideas are presented directly, as she thought them, on a prespeech level. These are her private thoughts. The fragmentary nature of the phrases is due to the fact that she is not concentrating on a specific topic. Rather, her mind is flowing freely on subjects that interest her. The three factors that control her associations are those usually found in the use of stream of consciousness.[34] In her thoughts, Lola is using her memory when she thinks of her dances with Bernardo; the sensorial has a place as well, with reference to her association with "light tobacco" (its odor, of course); and finally, she uses her imagination to give life to what has taken place between herself and Bernardo. We are also confronted in this passage by Romero's use of suspended coherence,[35] of which the phrase "don't trust, don't trust . . ." is illustrative. This expression is repeated a number of times, and being in the second person, eventually begins to disturb the reader. However, its meaning is fully appreciated when we remember that at an earlier time Lola mentioned that her girl friends "were telling her not to trust" Bernardo. When Lola repeats this phrase, she is remembering something that has meaning for her. Therefore, it needs no further elaboration if the author wishes to sustain the impression that what we read comes directly from her mind. The function of this phrase is to give to the reader something that will facilitate his better understanding of what has happened to Lola: she trusted Bernardo and had sexual relations with him.

A last narrative method to be considered is dialogue, of which Romero makes scant use.[36] There are some dialogues between two individuals (p. 199). On other occasions, Romero gives the words of only one character, as when Felipe Asencio is hit by a car (p. 149). An unusual type of dialogue is the one between Alicia and Ignacio. In their last "conversation," one can only hear what she says: what he states is simply understood (p. 59). One may conclude that all the narrative techniques used in *The Treadmill* try to characterize the personages from different avenues so that the reader may be fully aware of their many tribulations. The emphasis, as we have seen, falls directly or indirectly on the presentation of mental processes. It is in the mind that the themes of the novel come alive. The functional objective of narrative techniques in expressing themes is only partially successful because of the limitations inherent in those brief paragraphs that illustrate the use of the stream of consciousness.

V *Conclusion*

Thematically, *The Treadmill* focuses on the effects that an oppressive society exerts on the individual: a feeling of loneliness and the consequent evasion of life's many problems. Instead of placing the blame for these difficulties on specific institutions or individuals, their cause seems to be inherent in the human condition. Of importance, as well, is the theme of hope, although this aspect of *The Treadmill* seems somewhat forced, since its elaboration occurs mainly in the final pages of the novel. The image of the chain pump summarizes the thematic projection of Romero's first novel.

As far as techniques are concerned, *The Treadmill* (given the historical context of Spanish fiction in 1951) is a work which achieves its fundamental objectives. Through the simplicity of the framework he uses, Romero manages to reaffirm the fundamental problems of his characters by means of the novel's structure without losing its sense of unity. It is also evident that the author has attempted to choose the most appropriate narrative techniques to express the significant themes of *The Treadmill*. In this regard, the appearance of stream of consciousness is of special interest although it is not entirely successful, partly because of the length of the passages, and partly because of the manner in which they are employed. An even graver defect of the novel is the direct intervention of the narrator (or author) who offers subjective, personal opinions. The reader's awareness of what the narrator himself thinks about events in the work restricts the freedom of his characters and occasionally makes the artistic process entirely too obvious. It should be remembered, however, that the participation of the narrator is justifiable in the expression of man's duality, a major theme of the novel. *The Treadmill* is an auspicious first attempt by Romero. In it he displays a considerable talent as a narrator and offers promise of more important works in the future.

CHAPTER 4

A Period of Transition

C ARTA *de ayer (Letter from the Past)* and *Las viejas voces (The
Old Voices)* constitute an important link in Luis Romero's career
as a novelist. As we shall attempt to show, in these novels Romero
explored various thematic and artistic alternatives to the chronological episodes of *The Treadmill*. The author was concerned with the
recollection in the minds of the novels' protagonists of events in their
past, and although the novels are not particularly noteworthy, they
reflect Romero's efforts to probe more deeply into the characterization of his personages.

I *Toward a Dominant Perspective*

In 1953, after two years of silence, Luis Romero's second novel was
published by Editorial Planeta of Barcelona. *Letter from the Past* was
a step backward in Romero's career, inasmuch as he chose to
substitute the extreme and self-centered perspective of one character
for the balanced presentation of the collective protagonist of *The
Treadmill*. *Letter from the Past* recounts the ill-fated love of a young
writer and a woman old enough to be his mother. The story is told by
the male protagonist in the anguished prose of one who has abandoned the comforts and values of middle-class society to devote
himself to literature. After two brief, unplanned encounters, the
writer and woman become almost inseparable companions. Almost
from the beginning, they experience the joys of love and understanding, and soon the partners lose their sense of individuality and
independence as they realize that life is meaningless without one
another. But that their idyllic romance has a sad destiny is increasingly apparent even as their love binds them more inextricably
together.

Two factors lead to feelings of alienation and separation between
them. The difference in age which does not immediately concern

them begins to obsess both characters as they contemplate the time
when Claudia will no longer be attractive to her younger companion.
The other source of conflict is that the writer finds himself unable to
create because his sense of will and independence is destroyed
during his relationship with Claudia. In a like manner, Claudia is no
longer able to live alone and her dependence becomes such that
without him she almost dies. During the period of their separation,
the young man attempts futilely to escape his destiny through a brief
affair with an eighteen-year-old girl and by turning to excessive
drinking. However, he returns to Claudia when he learns of her
suffering.

Once again with her, the protagonist finds that his ability to write
creative and critical works is limited: he can only continue work on a
novel begun shortly prior to meeting Claudia. This novel, based on
the conflict of the love between a young student and a widow in her
forties, becomes increasingly autobiographical as its author's relationship with Claudia continues. The couple's own problems are
described in this novel, which becomes the story of their life
together. It is in the novel he is writing that the protagonist faces his
feelings toward Claudia and explores the alternatives that could solve
his dilemma. Finally he realizes that the inevitable conclusion to his
work is the only solution to the real-life predicament: the death of the
older woman. Having drunk many glasses of wine and cognac,
Romero's protagonist murders his mistress by opening the gas valve
in the kitchen as she lies asleep in the adjoining bedroom. The
murder occurs the very evening that she insists that he conclude his
novel, suggesting herself that the only proper conclusion would be
the murder of her fictional counterpart. In fact, she makes her lover's
action all the easier by taking a sleeping pill before retiring.[1]
Wandering through the streets after leaving Claudia, the writer
realizes what he has done and tries desperately but in vain to save
her. Ironically, the woman's death does not liberate the young man,
for her memory continues to haunt him. It is this memory that has
motivated him to write *Letter from the Past*, an analysis of previous
events: the confession of an obsessed mind.

Thematically speaking, *Letter from the Past* is a rather uncompli-
cated novel. Of foremost importance is the somewhat romantic
preoccupation with old age and its destructive effects, a theme
expressed vividly in the relationship between the protagonist and
Claudia, for almost immediately after falling in love they become

progressively aware that only a few years remain before she will cease to be attractive to him. Their relationship rapidly degenerates into a kind of cruel oppression, leading ultimately to murder.

To complement the obsession with advancing age, the poet, as he writes *Letter from the Past*, continues to reflect on the impossibility of reliving happy experiences. He refers to his youth as a period of innocence and happiness and recalls the joy of his honeymoon with Claudia. In a vain effort to relive the "good times," the pair return to Claudia's summer home with hopes of recovering some of the magic of their love for each other, but the attempt is inevitably a failure. As the couple become increasingly aware of their present without a future and their past which is forever lost, their unhappy destiny is sealed. Unfortunately the elaboration of the theme of time with respect to age and memory is excessively romantic and illogical in *Letter from the Past*. The protagonist's obsession with Claudia's eventual unattractiveness appears out of place so far in advance of her actual loss of physical appeal.[2] It does not seem necessary for two who love each other so deeply to dwell upon physical and moral destruction. Although their situation is possible, and in a sense may be representative of the alienation and lack of true communication which characterize contemporary literature, in the final analysis it is anachronistic and unreal.

Coexisting with the plethora of examples related to mortality and time, there is the suggestion of incest as a theme in *Letter from the Past*. In his description of Claudia, the young man often associates her with his aunt Lola, and even with his mother, realizing that there was something unhealthy about his relationship with them. On one occasion he describes his feeling for his mother as an "almost sickly love" (p. 35). Furthermore, the image of his mother is confused with memories of a maternal Claudia: "In the most remote evocations, the figure of Claudia is confused with that of my mother, and I feel small and inert in her arms, under her protection, and with the sensation that she was in me even before I existed" (pp. 127–28). Thus the association of Claudia with his aunt and mother is not merely based on a physical resemblance, for we find that at times the protagonist seeks maternal qualities in Claudia. After his break with Claudia and during their period of separation, it is significant that he courts Mary. He notices a physical similarity between the two women. He is pleased with Mary's curiosity about his poems. The girl's enthusiasm parallels Claudia's own interest in his works. Mary is not only a temporary substitute for Claudia, but may be seen as another woman with whom the narrator vaguely associates images of aunt Lola, his mother, and Claudia.

An important aspect of the relationship between the narrator-protagonist and Claudia is that he is unable to create original literature as long as he is with her. Every attempt to write is in vain, except for the autobiographical novel "Elisa." The protagonists of this novel within a novel, the young male student and Elisa, a widow in her forties, are described as "distantly related" (p. 53), and thus are involved in an incestuous affair. In addition, the novelist unconsciously combines images of Lola and Claudia in the creation of Elisa: "Still, the memory of my aunt Lola merged with that of Claudia in order to compose the figure of Elisa" (p. 138). The introduction and gradual superimposition of autobiographical characters in the novel suggest the theme of incest. The protagonist soon recognizes that he is writing the story of himself and Claudia and that, rather than being inventive, he is merely composing a thinly disguised fiction which eventually ceases to record the past and ultimately anticipates the future. When unable to write and when he obeys Claudia's suggestion that he finish the novel, the narrator is completely dominated by the woman.

During their separation, however, his strength and creative talents are partially restored, despite the fact that he continues to see Mary. His limited freedom is due, perhaps, to the fact that his love for Mary is never consummated sexually, and therefore incest is never committed. Could it be that the force which torments the protagonist is a feeling of guilt and the desire for self-punishment caused by incestuous feelings from his past; or is it the product of a late romanticism in which man submits himself totally to the influence and power of his companion? Any answer to this basic question is tentative and hypothetical, for despite the allusions to incest, the novel fails adequately to establish the cause of the protagonist's erratic and exaggerated behavior.

The reader of *Letter from the Past* is immediately confronted by the problem of viewpoint. Throughout the novel what prevails is the perspective of the protagonist,[3] who wishes to remember his activities with Claudia in order to recapture the feelings they had for one another. The protagonist freely blends in his narrative the present (in which he is writing) with the past. This interweaving of temporal planes creates confusion, for at times the reader does not know the exact moment at which a feeling or attitude was experienced. In *Letter from the Past* the young man wishes to explore the past for answers:

Even though the date lacks importance, or, at least, it seems that way to me now, during these years I have forced my memory to correlate facts, and I have hoped that chance, in one way or another, will clarify the exact day I met Claudia. I came to believe that after I knew the day something would be solved. Nevertheless, I have not been able to discern what is to be solved (p. 9).

In this passage, the protagonist expects some kind of solution to a unique and undefined problem as he explores his memory. This enigma could be the reason behind his actions. The title of the work, *Letter from the Past,* justifies our interpretation: this is a letter or message that the protagonist seeks from out of the past.

As a rule, the novel is descriptive, with first-person-singular perspective prevailing. The use of the first person is appropriate in the creation of the autobiographical effect for, undoubtedly, this is a novel of the ego: the views of the protagonist, his interests, are all that matter so far as his relation with Claudia is concerned. In many ways, *Letter from the Past* is the private dialogue of a man with himself and of that man with the reader. Beyond the use of the first-person perspective, there is little to be praised in *Letter from the Past.* The narrator constantly announces to the reader what is to happen later in the novel. These hints as to the outcome are in part motivated by the fact that the protagonist is writing a work which reflects his previous experiences: within memory one is free to associate events which took place at different times.

Already in the novel's second paragraph, the reader can perceive the emotional turbulence which is to follow:

Of course, it must have been during the last days of April or the first days of May. The year, I do remember without a possible doubt: it was in 1948. I am sure of this, even though, since then, my life has followed paths so different from what I expected . . . that my notion of time has become confused within me. (p. 9)

There are many examples of foreshadowing in the novel. For instance, as early as on page 65 we know of Claudia's death. We learn of the protagonist's desire to kill her on page 144, even though we do not become fully aware of his deed until page 275. As a result of this foreshadowing, the reader loses interest in a work which gives hints as to its outcome from its first page and consequently becomes too drawn out.[4]

Nor are the structure and style of *Letter from the Past* particularly strong. No specific reason regulates the division into chapters. Events taking place in one chapter are repeated in another. In fact, there is a prevailing tendency toward repetition in the novel, and even within a chapter a given idea is repeated many times without apparent need: "The idea to continue the novel was Claudia's. She told me to do it one day and I accepted . . . I am completely convinced of what I say: if the idea to continue the novel had not emanated from Claudia . . ." (p. 219). These two passages refer to a single event, and the second fails to add anything to the first. The effect of so many repetitions suggests a state of delirium, and from this angle, such an effort could be considered a positive aspect of the novel, being similar to the mental condition of the protagonist. However, abuse of this technique cancels out its advantages, making the reader weary of plodding his way through *Letter from the Past.*

Typical of the protagonist's means of expression is his hyperbolic vision of the cosmos:

I angrily exclaimed that I wouldn't wait a single minute more for a dessert or for all the desserts of my life if that meant having to listen to the foolishness of that bunch of idiots that he had just labelled gentlemen. (p. 53)

It was almost dawn when I fell asleep and I knew that Claudia had entered my life sweepingly and that always, for better or for worse, she would stay with me. (p. 36) When love kindles, it is like a storm with thunder and lightening, like a flood, like a waterfall. It invades the blood, the flesh, the faculties. . . . Since then I have felt that in a single kiss, all the power of the universe could be contained. (p. 78)

The exaggerations of the protagonist become so pompous that they remind the reader of the rhetorical excesses of the romantic movement. Also having romantic overtones are the frequent contradictory statements appearing in *Letter from the Past.* On page 62, for example, the narrator admits that it is impossible to describe a person (specifically Claudia), but then proceeds to do so on the same page. Such contradictions are troublesome to the reader, even if one accepts that they reflect the confused mind of the protagonist.

II   The Old Voices *as a Work of Reconciliation*

Two years after *Letter from the Past* was published, Luis Romero's third novel, *The Old Voices* (1955),[5] appeared. Here we observe a partial synthesis of those themes and techniques used by Romero in *The Treadmill* and *Letter from the Past*. *The Old Voices* is the story of a woman, Marta, who in her youth during the Civil War falls in love with a soldier. Soon after, she learns that her beloved has been killed in battle. Marta reacts with bitterness to this loss, blaming the world for its injustice, as she finds little understanding within her family. Part of her rebellious behavior takes the form of promiscuity, and Marta begins to live what her peers consider a loose life. It is this type of living that forces Marta to leave her conservative home town in disgrace and to become a prostitute in order to be able to survive in a harsh world. The novel, as a whole, consists of Marta's recollections. Undoubtedly, the past holds the key to her life of prostitution and solitude, for it is there that her life was shaped. It is with this background that Marta finally meets a man who promises to marry her. She accepts his offer, and her place in the bar is taken by another young woman; thus, Marta's role (her manner of living) will continue.

The title of the novel summarizes the technical means by which the themes of the novel are given form. The old voices referred to by the title are those memories from the past which prevail in the thoughts of Marta during most of the novel and which affect her emotionally throughout the novel. The protagonist of *The Old Voices* has two names: Marta and Luz. She had been called Marta before leaving her town and becoming a prostitute; she takes up the name once again as she establishes bonds with José, the man she is planning to marry. Thus, the name Marta is associated with purity and innocence, with happier moments in her life. The name Luz is in direct contrast with those traits attributed to Marta. Luz is her professional name in Barcelona, her name as a prostitute (p. 62). The presence of both names brings to the forefront the dichotomy of the character, her yesterday and her today. This distinction is fundamental to an understanding of the unhappiness experienced by Marta in Barcelona, her lack of satisfaction with her very existence there. All of this is seen very early in *The Old Voices:*

She calls them "dear," and that is a foolish word she has learned from the . . . motion pictures and that is used a lot by the girls who come to the bar. In reality, this is a somewhat childish vengeance, a small protest against the life she lives. (p. 8) She is nervous; she does not feel well. For a long time she has thought that she must do something to finish with this life before it finishes with her. But it is very difficult to decide anything. How will she solve, for instance, her economic problem? And it is not that alone, there are, as well, the customs and the need of companionship. At this time of day she wishes to come and submerge herself in this environment that is her own, in this place where her people are–even though she doesn't even appreciate them, although many of those meeting here are even disliked by her–. In order to replace one habit, she needs to create another. Outside these walls she lacks friends. Here, at least, there are people who love her. . . . (pp. 60–61)[6]

The previous quotations allow us to perceive Marta's unhappiness. The second quotation also adds to the reasons why she feels this way: her profession is not the fundamental element in her negative attitude; rather, her basic problem is her solitude. The world which surrounds Marta is alien and meaningless to her (p. 109). The major problem is that no one is interested in her as a human being (p. 75).

Just as important as Marta's solitude—a reflection of mankind's solitude—there is something else that increases her unhappiness. She realizes that the years are going by and that old age is advancing upon her:

Perhaps in another city of the world there is a girl with a smooth forehead who could be called Marta, and in a bar somewhere another woman called Luz may have a forehead as [unlined] as hers was ten years ago. But neither that Marta nor that Luz will be her. She will be dead, she will no longer be. . . . (p. 31)

The combination within Marta of her fear of the passing of time and her solitude impels her to act in many ways. Thus, she becomes interested in Manuel, a man who reminds her of her youth and who may end her solitude with his companionship.

Marta tries to escape the reality surrounding her by her mental return to the past, to a period in her life which she misses. When returning to the past, Marta behaves in two ways: she idealizes this period by inventing events that did not take place, and she remembers it as it was, as something lost that she would like to recapture. Both approaches to the past are forms of evasion. Marta's first type of behavior is relatively infrequent in the novel. When it does occur she creates a reality that, had it taken place, would have saved her from her present situation:

This afternoon she had thought that in her city there could live a Marta Alvarez thirty-seven years old, daughter of the solicitor Don Justo Alvarez, sister of Charo and Asunción. A Marta Alvarez who during the war was a nurse and had fun as the other girls did and who had a boyfriend, a lieutenant . . . who enjoyed only eight days of furlough. . . . Pedro was killed and Marta's desperation was such that she believed she would die of sorrow. But her father and mother who loved her deeply, and her two sisters, Asunción and Charo, showed so much interest and sensitivity toward her that little by little time made her forget that unlucky love, that, after all, only lasted eight days and had no physical and spiritual transcendence beyond that passionate kiss on the porch. (pp. 109–10)[7]

The second type of evasion prevails in the first chapter of the novel ("The Bar"). It is from this kind of evasion that the reader becomes aware of an oppressive social and cosmic reality that is responsible for Marta's life in Barcelona. At least, this is the way Marta sees things as she evaluates her father (a tyrant), her mother (frightful), her sisters (indifferent), and society (critical of her love affairs).[8] Marta's complaints, however, go well beyond those who surrounded her. To Marta, it was unjust for Pedro, her lover, to have died. In her view, something had been taken from her. Thus, another theme of *The Old Voices* is life's inherent injustice:

After receiving the news she remained crushed. In her home they thought she was sick and she did not change their impression for she could not tell them the truth either. She stayed in bed for three days. It is during those days that a feeling of rebelliousness began to germinate in her spirit, a feeling that would explode later on. She rebelled against God. Then she was angry with Pedro for having abandoned her this way, for having died, for not being capable of overcoming that death which was to separate them forever. (p. 199)

A last theme to be considered is also related to Marta's past. At first she views her past with a certain longing, a sadness because she cannot relive the happier moments of her life. However, her attitude changes during the course of the novel. Marta realizes that it is impossible to return to what has been, partly because her outlook on life has changed:

In the portraits, in the letters, there is a sense of anguish and inevitability that is better forgotten, because one lives from day to day and only the present exists as reality. The past is nothing more than the material with which people have painfully gone about creating and developing themselves. The saddest

thing is that Pedro wore pointed sideburns, and despite all her efforts to
convince herself that in those days it must have been in style, the image of the
portrait becomes ridiculous and loses the evocative majesty which she would
like it to preserve. (p. 40)

The picture of Pedro, so loved by Marta, wounds her because she
realizes that he is but an image from the past. The impossibility of
recovering the past is the theme which dominates the second chapter
of the novel ("The City"). Marta realizes that her home town has
changed almost completely and that nothing seems to be just as it was
during her childhood there. It is then that she becomes aware that the
past has died forever: "But her father, her mother, her sisters, even
she herself, cannot be there. They remained in another point in time,
in a stagnant backwater which is dying, which is almost dead" (p.
232). A related aspect of *The Old Voices* is the already-mentioned
attempt to project Marta's problems on others, and thus to universalize the themes of loneliness, the anxiety of aging, social and cosmic
injustice, and the impossibility of reliving the past. This is the thrust
of the final chapter of the novel ("Absence"). The narrator returns to
the bar, this time without the presence of Marta, to present life as it
goes on there without her. Essentially nothing has changed, and all
the "regulars" of the bar reveal characteristics which were either part
of Marta's personality or of her condition. The narrative point of view
which predominates in this section is that of the omniscient author
who chronicles the tedium and inescapable boredom trapping the
characters of the bar. The final paragraph of the work introduces a
new character, who because of her particular characteristics—two
names, a similar background, and probable illicit relations in her
past—becomes the new Marta:

Cuca sits down at the extreme end of the bar. She arrived in Barcelona two
months ago, and a girl named Rita who lives in the same boarding house as
she brought her to this bar. In reality, her name isn't Cuca, but Josefina. In
her home town all the young men courted her, but for two years now she
hasn't had any boyfriends. The one she had, who was handsome, belonged to
one of the richest families in the province. Her father forbade her to see him,
but at nightfall they would meet, secretly, in the park. All the girls of the town
envied her good luck. (pp. 273–74)

Of course the themes of *The Old Voices* are nothing new. In *The
Treadmill* Romero sought to express human problems and concerns

by means of a series of scenes in which many characters experience and suffer alike. In *Letter from the Past*, the emphasis is strictly on the problems of the novel's protagonist. *The Old Voices* represents Luis Romero's first attempt to combine a well-developed characterization of an individual (Marta) with the projection of a collective reality as experienced by those who frequent the bar.

As previously stated, the novel is divided structurally into three chapters of varying length, each corresponding to one stage of the thematic development of the novel. The first of these, "The Bar," presents the daily visits of Marta. This division which comprises more than half the novel is subdivided into sections, generally one for each nightly appearance there. Scenes of the "present" as Marta con-templates the "regulars" and the visitors to the familiar atmosphere of the bar are mixed together with her memories of events and circumstances from her "former" life. The second chapter, "The City," basically presents Marta's visit to her home town. Repeated contrast between her recollections of the town and the reality of the present during her visit characterizes this division of the novel. Except for brief reflections on her recent departure from Barcelona, chapter two is divided as is the first, between memories of her youth and her present activities. The third chapter "Absence," the shortest in *The Old Voices*, is a return to the Barcelona hangout, this time, however, without Marta. Routine activities and regular clients are shown in Romero's efforts to universalize problems previously seen only in terms of the protagonist.

Two structural weaknesses are evident in *The Old Voices*. First of all, the attempt to express universal themes in the third chapter is abrupt and awkward. It would have been much more effective to develop this aspect of the novel from the beginning. The second problem is similar to the first. Marta's union with the American at the end of the novel receives only minor elaboration. Even more curious is that such an important element of the plot and one which establishes the theme of the futility of reliving the past, is not presented dramatically within the novel. We learn of their courtship mostly in retrospect (chapter two).

The most significant structural feature of the novel, however, is the continuous alternating rhythm from past to present, present to past, in *The Old Voices*. Such movement is predominant in the first two chapters of the novel as Marta transports herself mentally from her present circumstances into the past. The "old voices" beckon her to seek refuge in the past and to escape reality, but ultimately Marta understands that her only hope for happiness lies in a present filled with plans and hopes for the future.

With regard to narrative point of view, *The Old Voices* offers no innovation compared to the author's earlier works. Indirect interior monologue is used throughout the first two chapters, for it enables Marta to present her personal problems and to recall her past as it consciously or subconsciously relates to the present (p. 15). Romero utilizes this point of view in *The Old Voices* with considerable success as a vehicle for the expression of mental activity. Indirect interior monologue is discontinued, however, in the final part. In Marta's absence, an omniscient narrator describes what each character does and thinks as he focuses his camera lens on the persons who frequent the bar. Limited amounts of dialogue in *The Old Voices* (pp. 192 and 205) are used effectively to represent what takes place in the present. By not depending entirely on Marta's imagination and interpretation of reality, her ideas are seen from a different angle and may be examined in a more rational and understandable context.

III *Conclusion*

From the presentation of the influence exerted by an oppressive society on the individual, so prevalent in *The Treadmill*, Luis Romero took his readers to the somewhat romantic dilemmas of the protagonist of *Letter from the Past*. The difference between these two works is not merely thematic. While in *The Treadmill* many characters are viewed in an attempt to discover a common denominator among them and humanity, in *Letter from the Past* we have the dominant mono-perspective of a protagonist who attributes cosmic proportions to his own personal and limited problems. It is safe to say that in *Letter from the Past* the reader witnesses a retrogression from Romero's novelistic achievements of *The Treadmill: Letter from the Past* is totally lacking in a search for new means of expression. It is in this context that Romero's third novel appeared. The significance of *The Old Voices* is that it blends principal themes (for instance, solitude, society's oppression of the individual, and the preoccupation with the passing of time and its effects upon man) and techniques (i.e., the combination of generic and individual perspectives) that appeared in *The Treadmill* and *Letter from the Past*. Thus, *The Old Voices* is a work of reconciliation; it epitomizes a period of transition in Romero's career as a novelist. Fortunately, out of this stage in his development as a writer, Luis Romero emerged better aware of his role as an artist.

CHAPTER 5

The Capsular Novel

*L*OS otros *(The Others)* and *La corriente (The Current)* represent the end of a cycle in Luis Romero's narratives because of their themes, the presence of a common setting, and the fragmented form of the novel.

I *Existential Dilemmas*

The plot of *The Others* (1956) revolves around the attempted holdup of a company officer by a man who has resorted to violence in order to escape his life of poverty and despair. The action takes place in less than a day, from the early morning hours when the thief awakes, to late evening when his body is identified. There are, however, other characters in *The Others* whose lives are touched by the events of the day. José Mateo, an accountant, is seriously wounded by the criminal. The factory owner is studied as he contemplates the crime and its resultant inconveniences. There is Carmela, the thief's wife, who has been a victim all her life, and Mr. Portaló, the company bill collector, who is seen as he watches over his wife on her deathbed. Minor characters include the guards who happen onto the scene of the crime, and Nuria, a company secretary who falls in love with José Mateo. Also significant is the tavern owner, who believes in the authority of the law but sympathizes with the unfortunate circumstances of the poor and oppressed.

The major thematic thrust of *The Others* is aptly described in the novel's epigraph: "Come, let us go down, and there confuse their language, that they may not understand one another's speech (Genesis 11:7)" (p. 7).[1] This passage suggests the inability of men and women to communicate meaningfully with each other, the central problem which is the essence of *The Others*. Furthermore, the book's title subtly reinforces the same principle, the egocentric nature of all human beings that limits their ability and desire to communicate effectively, as if saying "my" view is correct, that of "the others" is of no account.

In the novel Romero proceeds to create a comprehensive vision of the world via the presentation of contrasting, sometimes contradictory and almost always absolute viewpoints of the same events as interpreted by different characters. For example, the collector (Mr. Portaló), the factory owner, and the accountant José Mateo Mora offer very different views as to their relative importance to the same company. Mr. Portaló sees himself as a valuable asset to the firm:

The boss likes him; he already worked for his [the boss's] father when they had only a modest engine repair shop. Now they've given him a good position in the enterprise; he's the one they trust, the bill collector. And today definitely is Saturday, the last day of the month, and it's time to go to the bank to get the money for the payroll. Now they'll have to send someone else. Maybe the owner or the manager will go, since they have cars. (p. 31)

A contrasting opinion of Mr. Portaló's value is expressed by José Mateo, who, as an accountant, considers himself superior in rank and prestige to his fellow employee:

This is plain stupid; because the collector doesn't show up, they send another employee in his place. They don't have the right, and if they try it again, he'll refuse. The only thing missing is for them to fit him with the uniform jacket and cap. Oh well, this time he'll keep quiet and do what they want; but an accountant shouldn't have to substitute for a mere collector. (p. 75)

In direct opposition to the views of the employees is the personal attitude of the company owner, who considers himself an adversary to his workers. He is convinced that they work little and care less about the company's success:

All the weight of the work falls on his shoulders: to struggle constantly with clients, creditors, workers. Nobody gives him a cent, no; he earns his money through his own efforts, his work, his industrial and business instincts. Neither the manager nor the engineer nor the foremen would do anything without him. (p. 37)

Communication barriers extend, however, beyond the stratified hierarchy of the company. In the following passage the thief shows a concern and love for Carmela that he is never able to express openly to her:

But again he's fed up with working all day to earn thirty-two pesetas, and he's tired of breathing sawdust and of seeing Carmela going around in mended stockings. Carmela won't be like his mother. Carmela won't shrivel up among sighs and dirty clothes, she won't wear kerchiefs in winter, nor will she get old while chained to a sewing machine. (p. 13)

Unfortunately, Carmela herself remains passive and uncommunicative before his silence. Thus the pattern of alienation and loneliness is continued:

She would have liked to say something to him, but he was more locked up than ever in his almost hostile silence. He must not love her; if he loved her, he wouldn't do that, that which he's going to do today, something she doesn't really understand, but which nevertheless frightens her. (p. 64)

Since all the characters are unable to perceive and much less understand the existence of other points of view regarding any particular event or circumstance, they are totally frustrated by the impossibility of meaningful communication.

In fact, the individual in *The Others* discovers that he is completely alone. The world is quickly divided into an endless variation of the same dichotomy: on the one hand, the individual and his interests, and on the other, the rest of the world. The attitude of the thief, who knows he is being pursued, exemplifies the theme of human loneliness and isolation:

On one side is he, and he alone, and on the other, the entire city, the whole world. (p. 106)

Again he shows it [the gun] to him menacingly. He pants; if he faints, the hostility of the taxi-driver will vent itself on him. And the hostility of a million and a half citizens will crush him. There was that obstinate triangle, and the gray guards with short barreled rifles in hand came running as fast as they could. (p. 115)

Of course *The Others* is not limited thematically to the problem of man's lack of communication and its painful results. The work also provides severe criticism of a society in which the working masses are exploited. The most extreme condemnation of the system is expressed by the thief, whose views of class struggle are apparent in the following passage:

He's tired of making others rich with his work. Someone with money puts a few wretches together and makes them work. He pays them no more than

what is required to keep them from dying of hunger or cold; that is, the
minimum for them to maintain their strength and thus be able to keep
working. Then the guy, who already had money, makes even more. Now he
can live in a warm home, his wife is well dressed. . . . (pp. 13–14)
    Yes, they'll change the world, but meanwhile what he's going to do is
change his life, which is more urgent. Change his life before Carmela's skin
becomes wrinkled and he loses his health; before a machine mutilates him
irreparably or they throw him in jail for knocking the boss on the head the day
he hears him say that workers live better than he. (p. 15)

Evidence of social injustice pervades the entire novel, as virtually all
the characters are in some way shown as victims of their own inability
to understand themselves and others. It is no wonder that society is
viewed as an impersonal, oppressive force in their lives. When José
Mateo complains of his almost hopeless struggle to better his
position, his supervisor—who defends the "haves" and not the
"have-nots"—ironically explains that the system can succeed only if
those like José Mateo accept their miserable lot:

He assures [José Mateo] that if they were to raise wages, commerce and
industry would be ruined, and, if that weren't enough, it would produce
inflation again, as in countries where high salaries are paid. [José Mateo] fails
to comprehend what good the prosperity of a few abstract entities such as
"industry" and "commerce" and the "nation" is, if, on the other hand,
people, citizens, live poorly. . . . He suspects that those abstract words . . .
aren't as abstract as he thought, and that behind such words one finds those
with well-dressed wives, those who own cars and spend their summers at the
beach; in a word, those who object to José Mateo Mora's earning a wage
increase. (pp. 95–96)

Lack of communication and comprehension, loneliness, and social
criticism are all interrelated in *The Others* by the successful use of
irony.[2] The disparity between one character's point of view and that
of "the others," apparent in José Mateo's conversation with his
foreman, is even more powerfully evident in the egocentric, pompous reflections of the factory owner as he absolves himself of
responsibility for not having visited José Mateo, and vainly overesti-
mates his own importance:

And he didn't even have time to go to visit him in the hospital to express his
admiration to him, something which if it were to take place, would
undoubtedly be of great comfort to the dying [man]. (p. 145)

Not only do his views reveal the barriers to communication, but through irony they are used to attack the insensitive, hypocritical, and materialistic socioeconomic class which he represents.[3]

II *A Day in Barcelona*

With *The Others* Luis Romero continues a predominant characteristic of *The Treadmill:* the presentation of reality in a fragmented fashion. As with his more famous first novel, *The Others* is divided into many short chapters which place emphasis on the activities, thoughts and conversations of many characters. However, in *The Others* there is more elaboration of the characters, for a number of these chapters are dedicated to individual histories. In a sense, what we have is a jigsaw puzzle that is put together the day the thief assaults José Mateo Mora. Thus, all the chapters resemble pieces that contribute to the creation of the characters of the novel. In addition, this structural fragmentation heightens the breakdown of communication between the characters: it serves to reassert that each man is a different and separate unit.

Of interest as well is that the thief of *The Others*, the protagonist of the novel, has had a previous existence in *The Treadmill*. In Romero's first novel he was the son of Mercedes, the maid of Jorge Mas. There is little difference in the presentation of her son in *The Treadmill* and *The Others*. In both novels he is bitter because of his poverty and driven to crime as the only escape from his sad situation. In *The Others*, he makes references to previous crimes and, above all, to his encounter with a man (Felipe Asencio) who almost refused to surrender his money to him. Mercedes's son is in both works a poor carpenter ready to kill or be killed as he desperately attempts to improve his lot. Thus, what we have is the creation of a world of fiction a la Galdós which transcends the boundaries of a given novel yet adds authenticity to Luis Romero's creation. Facilitating this process is the fact that both *The Treadmill* and *The Others* take place in Barcelona. This common setting further contributes to the book's versismilitude.

The Others offers the reader a day in Barcelona. When this time limitation is spread over the many chapters used for the presentation of each character, the reader realizes that time has acquired an unusual density in the novel. As a result, it is justifiable for the reader to feel weary as the problems confronted by the characters are described in detail as if everything were occurring in slow motion. An

The Capsular Novel

The Capsular Novel61

excellent example is the presentation of those moments after the thief orders José Mateo to surrender the money he is carrying:

> A second of hesitation. At the door of the establishment appears the bartender with a frightened face and he withdraws immediately to the interior. He [the thief] has to move slightly to avoid any aggression that may come from inside the tavern. He [the bartender] was a man lacking in will power, badly shaven. . . . He advances a step without hesitation. They are now close to one another. The man with the dark suit [José Mateo] has made a slight movement with his eyebrows, as if trying to return to the reality from which surprise had taken him. His eyes acquire brilliancy, fear, hesitation. (p. 109)

The fatigue to which we are referring responds to technical needs of *The Others*. [4] It is through this feeling that we are able to comprehend fully what the thief experiences in his life and, primarily, what he feels as he vainly seeks refuge after being wounded during the holdup:

> A man stops by his side; he can hardly see him and does not know if he is old or young. He repels him with a gesture and the other continues on his way. With a convulsion he lets go of the lamppost and goes a few additional steps.
> He will not arrive, now for sure he will not arrive, and Carmela was waiting for him at the end of this street, and there [waiting for him] were doctors and a bed, and perhaps the police would have left him alone because at the end of the street there was something that he would not be able to reach because he lacks strength to go on and to reach the end of this street.
> He falls on the ground and feels pain in his face. He sits up supporting himself on his right elbow and he feels his face. It is covered with blood and dust. He crawls on his belly; he can do no more. (pp. 229–30)

Romero's use of indirect interior monologue gives a sense of vitality to the characters of *The Others*. It allows the reader to witness the character's private thoughts as conveyed by an omniscient narrator:

> He turns at the first intersection and goes slowly. He remembers in this instant that as he paid for his [drink], he took his left hand out of his pocket and that the waiter could have observed that he was missing a phalanx from a finger. The police works in a subtle fashion, and the city, even though it is big, is always a limited space, a mousetrap after all. (p. 85)

While the omniscient narrator serves the reader as a guide, he at times takes the liberty of expressing his opinion about what takes

place. This, in turn, detracts from the autonomy of the novel, creating
the impression that the narrator does not feel that the characters can
with their deeds alone convince the reader of the magnitude of their
problems:

> These are the industrial districts—broad backs of a rich and unmerciful
> city—the districts precisely from which the wealth of this city emanates. . . .
> These are the forgotten districts, where the people from downtown never
> come, unless they have located here their industry or their charity. (p. 49)
> There is a moment of confusion and the owner stretches his hand toward
> him, a hand that the other shakes. This is the first time that they have shaken
> hands and neither of the two knows very well why he has done this. *Perhaps
> they have come to believe this business of trust.* (p. 78, our italics)

In the first example the narrator moralizes about the poor districts of
Barcelona, while in the second he states his belief that between the
owner and José Mateo there could be no trust. The narrator's
personal perspective intrudes between the reader and the novel in
both instances.[5]

It should be clarified that the use of the indirect interior
monologue, the perspective of an omniscient narrator, and dialogue
(e.g., pp. 23 and 123) in *The Others* is due in part to Luis Romero's
desire to provide a more profound vision of reality. Each means of
expression serves as an avenue facilitating the understanding of the
characters and their deeds. Although the omniscient perspective is
abused, this same perspective serves as a background to the action
we are witnessing. Omniscience is in evidence when the reader
discovers the attitude of Mateo's landlady toward one of her tenants
(pp. 23–24). By allowing us to know Doña Anita's feelings, the
narrator is placing Mateo in a realistic environment and is, consequently, giving verisimilitude to the novel. When the omniscient
perspective is discriminating and functional, it becomes an artistic
asset within *The Others*.

A final aspect to be considered in our study of *The Others* is the
feeling of continuity derived from the first paragraph of the novel:
"Once again he has awakened with the sensation of having jumped.
. . . Now, against the panes of the window a pale light rests. Dawn
has come" (p. 11). The expression "once again" and its association
with "dawn" implies the recurrence of an event. Thus the novel is
giving us just one day even though it is recognized that this day is only
a segment of a wider period of time. The action takes place within a
large chronology of which we are dimly aware. As in *The Treadmill*,

Romero communicates implicitly that we are witnessing an incident drawn from a more ample reality. Conceivably, the experiences of the characters of *The Others* are as representative as those of their counterparts in *The Treadmill* because both works provide selective views of the dilemmas of mankind.

III   *The End to a World of Fiction*

With *The Current* (1962),[6] Luis Romero returns to the techniques of the fragmented, capsular novel that were marks of his success in *The Treadmill* and *The Others*. *The Current* gives final touches to a fictional world of a host of characters, most of whom were first introduced in *The Treadmill*. In fact, to many critics Romero's new work was primarily a continuation of the Nadal Prize–winning novel, depicting the anguished lives of its characters as seen ten years later.[7] This view is essentially correct, it being understood that new characters are introduced and that not all of the characters of *The Treadmill* reappear in *The Current*. However, Romero not only ties these two novels together, but uses characters and situations from *The Others* and *The Old Voices*. Although independent from the other novels and complete in itself, and although it does not require that a reader be familiar with the previous works, *The Current* synthesizes and closes a cycle of Romero's fiction. It is, above all, the presentation of a panoramic vision of modern Barcelona.

As was the case in *The Treadmill*, the "plot" of *The Current* consists of a series of slices of life. Although certain characters are treated in more than one chapter (unlike *The Treadmill*), no protagonist exists other than metropolitan Barcelona of the early sixties. In its title Romero synthesizes the major thrust of the novel: life is a current that incessantly advances and in which human lives are swept along unwillingly or at least unconsciously.[8] The importance of the metaphorical title may further be seen in the fact that the novel includes many characters from previous works. Thus the vital movement of life which begins and develops in them is continued in *The Current*. A variety of characters reappear in *The Current*, ten years after many were first seen in *The Treadmill*, and five years after the unsuccessful robbery of a factory payroll in *The Others*. While it is not true that *The Current* is merely an extension of *The Treadmill* or *The Others*, the presence of common characters creates a tightly-knit fictional world.

The lives of some of the most interesting personages of *The*

Treadmill are reviewed ten years after they were originally presented. The list is extensive and includes the homosexual Arístides,
Paco, Francisco, Gallardo, Alvaro, "El Sardineta" (formerly a tramp
and now a respectable barber), González and Elvira, Alicia and
Ignacio Dalmau (now married), and their maid. Also appearing for
the second time are the pathetic cuckold Esteban, the flirt Hortensia
and her replacement on the hospital night shift (Berta), Berta's father,
an old and failing Don Raimundo, Pepe Rovira, Lola, Felipe Asencio,
the taxi-driver Manuel, and Llorach. Alicia's brother Quique, once
an artist, now is a businessman. The desperate old woman selling
sandwiches in *The Treadmill* has succeeded in accumulating enough
savings to assure that financial security which is her only obsession.

Of primary importance are those characters who appear more often
throughout the novel. These include Roberto, now "home" in
Barcelona after spending ten years in South America, who seeks a
Spanish wife. Industrialist Juan Anchorena Zubigaray, nicknamed
"Juanchu," visits his mistress whenever possible and provides her
with the money to run her own small business. Raquel finds herself
unable to abandon her lover, Jorge Mas, while at the same time her
husband, Santiago, is worried about a possible cancer. Trini (the
nickname of Vicenta) continues her struggle to survive in a world
which has offered her few advantages.[9]

Two characters from *The Others* reappear in *The Current*. Although of minor importance, they serve to solidify the fictional
universe of Romero's Barcelona. In *The Current* we meet one of the
guards involved in the holdup,[10] who now discusses the incident with
his new partner. Mr. Portaló, the bill collector who has lived alone
since the death of his wife, joins Berta's parents in a nightly card
game. In addition, references are made to Portaló's ex-employer, the
wealthy owner of the engine factory who realizes huge profits with an
inferior product while minimizing workers's salaries. And characters
recall Carlos's bar, the scene of most of the action of *The Old Voices*.

Thus the movement of the current of life continues from one novel
to the next, bearing witness to vital human problems which characterize each one: solitude, the aimlessness and emptiness of life, lack
of communication, the effects of aging, and social injustice. All these
problems are so closely related as to provide a total effect exceeding
the sum total of the parts. The individual feels alone and isolated
because he cannot communicate effectively with those around him,
nor can he overcome the destructive combination of the indifference
and abuses of the society in which he lives. His lack of direction is

a product of his solitude: he does not know whether or not his job or activities are at all worthwhile. And meanwhile, crippled by indecision and uncertainty about personal values and goals, he must face the fact that he is growing older and that every passing day will be irretrievably lost.

But despite the atmosphere of anxiety and tension, the final chapter of *The Current* is filled with optimism and hope. As in *The Treadmill*, the light of the new day suggests a possibility that the quality of life may improve. A wave of optimism, of "light at the end of the tunnel," permeates the end of the chapter in which the author refers to the generation represented by the yet unborn child of Vicentina:

> This generation will endure a moment of terror; when their children have reached adulthood they will be out of the tunnel, breathing clean air. In the brightness of the sun, the terrors will seem superficial. If it weren't this way, if they weren't convinced that this were so, how could they even have children?, how could anyone be happy at their birth? One must be prepared to challenge the nightmare, to bear the weight of all the fear on one's shoulders so that one's children are born free from fear. It's absolutely necessary to believe that it will be this way. (p. 312)
>
> It's daytime, full daylight. The sun which will shed its light throughout the city, illuminating even its farthest reaches, is about to rise. (p. 313)

IV *Narrative Density*

Time and action are closely related in *The Current*. The novel takes place during one day. However, this chronological limitation is compensated by the memories of the characters. Thus, the limited time span of the work is expanded by means of density of action. Compactness of action is achieved by the presentation of simultaneous events, as can be detected in Roberto's casual meeting with Arístides:

> He drinks the last drops in his glass with a disconsolate expression. Arístides puts to his lips the red, transparent liquid.
> —Give me another double.
> Along the Gracia promenade, now illuminated by a brilliant sun, parade the automobiles with their shining colors as if they were a rapid and fantastic cavalcade. Young and well-dressed women, men who go or come from their duties, ladies who walk their children or dogs. . . . Life is out there, in the men and women, in the children, in the dogs, in the automobiles. . . . (p. 82)

The density in the above passage is illustrative of this phenomenon throughout *The Current*. Romero creates the impression that what we are witnessing is a partial view of the river of life. There are aspects of that "river" not discussed in the novel, lives not mentioned, which, nevertheless, *The Current* allows us to perceive as existing.

Even though the chronological boundaries of *The Current* give the impression of going well beyond the one day during which the novel takes place, this does not mean that *The Current* lacks unity or is diluted in a sea of time. On the contrary, the structure of the chapters provides cohesiveness to the work. *The Current's* organic unity emanates from the fact that most of the characters appear in more than one chapter.[11] Along with the reappearance of the personages, another unifying element is the small talk which, so far as its content is concerned, tends to overlap from individual to individual, even though the characters have little in common. Examples of this technique include the many references to Rodrigo and his unexpected death (pp. 58, 79, 209, 281, 285, 286). Using their own perspectives, rich and poor, friends and strangers, speak of this death. The reference to Rodrigo by such a diverse group is logical, for he was both a prominent citizen and an outcast of Barcelona, a city of which all the characters are inhabitants.

Among the narrative techniques used in *The Current* are indirect[12] and direct interior monologues. The latter device is used in that mental "dialogue" which Raimundo sustains with those who surround him:

> You and the smoke may go to hell; I have smoked numerous Turkish and Egyptian cigarettes, and that is without counting Havana cigars, for I didn't do without them either, and you, [poor excuse for a man] are coming to ask me if the smoke bothers me. Do you really think we are made of the same stuff? You are my nephew by chance and thank God we are not alike even in the whites of our eyes; only milligrams of my blood are in yours, a small speratozoid. . . . (p. 147)

Another narrative technique is the dialogue. At times it serves to vitalize, to place in a real context, those thoughts of the characters which are expressed by means of the indirect interior monologue:

> —Do you know who I saw yesterday? I wanted to tell you and then I forgot.
> —. . . ?
> —It was Roberto.
> —Which Roberto?

—What do you mean by which Roberto? That friend of yours who used to come to the office and who emigrated. . . . (pp. 120–21)

A final aspect to be considered with regard to the interior monologues is the author's omniscience in them. For example, "Each minute behind schedule is an offense against the pocket from whence the salaries came. . . . By dealing with distinguished people one gains breeding; for a number of years *Sardineta* has liked to choose his acquaintances" (p. 17). In this quotation the narrator blends his judgment with the thoughts of *Sardineta* to facilitate their expression. This omniscience was deliberate on the part of Romero ("to a certain extent I am within each character. I intervene"[13]) and is not always effective. At times the narrator uses his omniscience to extremes as he evaluates individuals and circumstances:

> González is not an acute observer; withdrawn in his problems and obsessed by his work, he hardly concerns himself with others unless they require his attention because of a specific event or circumstances. *He would excuse himself by saying that he does not have time to waste and he wouldn't be far wrong in stating this.* (p. 23, our italics)

While speaking about González, the narrator indicates that he is not a profound observer and proceeds immediately to imagine how González would answer this accusation. As the narrator anticipates González's position, he is justifying it. Such examples detract from the work because all means of expression in the novel should function to facilitate the presentation of the characters. The visualization of the personages' traits is hampered when frequently the reader cannot distinguish between the thoughts of a given character and those of the narrator.[14] The narrator's intervention is not, as we have indicated, unusual in Romero's novels. We have pointed out a number of times the lack of distance between the creator and his creations.

Adding to the technical complexity of *The Current* is the double perspective from which some things are presented. This technique reaffirms existing differences between the points of view of two or more individuals as they interpret the reality which surrounds them. For instance, a character may see his obesity as attractive, as a symbol of his maturity, while the same condition is considered a defect by someone else:

> He sees himself in that mirror which is to the left of the counter. . . . He is not unhappy with his appearance as a mature man, obviously obese, but with

a powerful and respectable look, those are the characteristics that attract
women. (p. 55–56)
    He is capable of supposing that he could win her because of his handsome
face. And what a gut he has! (p. 56)

The presence of many perspectives on a given subject facilitates the
development of *The Current's* themes,[15] lending verisimilitude to
what the novel portrays.
    Also of importance in the creation of a realistic environment in *The
Current* are the many references to Barcelona and to names of
historical individuals and events (i.e., Américo Castro, Fidel Castro,
the struggle for independence in the Congo). It is obvious that by
making the novel part of the real world, Romero is facilitating our
acceptance of what is said in *The Current*. This feeling is further
enhanced by the use of vulgar jokes which blend well with what is
taking place in the novel. Thus, when the owner of a factory is trying
to determine, by discussing the workers' personal traits, who among
his employees wrote political graffiti on the walls of his business, he is
told of "El Pencas," a man who is capable of such a deed if the
subject is pornographic:

    —I see that you know him already. He is the one they call "El Pencas." I
don't think that politics concern him. You see, if what had appeared was a
naked woman, or . . . well, you understand what I am saying, I would suspect
him.
    —But perhaps he did it as a joke . . .
    —As a joke he would have drawn something dirty, with hair in its place and
everything. Pardon me for speaking this way. (p. 126)

The humor shown in this passage makes the reader an active
participant in what is described insofar as his appreciation of the joke
is concerned.

V *Conclusion*

    Thematically and technically *The Others* and *The Current* con-
clude a period in Luis Romero's literary production. Both works place
emphasis on the many existential problems faced by modern man and
present reality as fragmented in nature but nevertheless continuous.
The reappearance of characters from *The Treadmill* and *The Old
Voices* in *The Others* and primarily in *The Current* contributes to the
creation of an autonomous world by allowing this body of fiction to

acquire verisimilitude. With *The Others* and *The Current* Luis Romero has successfully explored many of the artistic possibilities of the capsular novel.

CHAPTER 6

Other Narratives

U P to this point in our study of Luis Romero we have considered a number of his works either separately (as in the case of *The Treadmill*) or in combination with other novels sharing similar characteristics. Our objective in this chapter is to relate works that at times show common thematic and artistic traits, but as a rule are too diverse to constitute a cohesive unit. The first six sections treat collections of short stories, *Esas sombras del trasmundo (Shadows from Beyond)* and *Tudá*. Section VII analyzes Romero's sixth novel, *La noche buena (Christmas Eve)*, while sections VIII and IX deal respectively with "La noria de los recuerdos" ("The Treadmill of Memories") and five short stories published between 1958 and 1972.

I Shadows from Beyond

Shadows from Beyond, Romero's first collection of brief fiction, appeared in 1957.[1] This volume of twenty-one short stories represents Romero's first attempt in this genre. The title of the volume suggests the unifying element of the collection: a vision of human beings who experience in one way or another aspects of the phantasmagorical world of the "hereafter," of life beyond the grave or at least beyond the realm of normal human experience. The "shadows" are perceived generally in two ways: from the point of view of a protagonist who continues to "live" even after his physical death, and through the eyes of the living who in some way encounter the "other" world.

More specifically, the stories are linked by themes and narrative techniques prevalent in Romero's novels. We should add, however, that his treatment of death allows for certain thematic and stylistic innovations. The nature of death is the primary theme of the book, but Romero is also concerned with the feeling of loneliness and marginality which characterizes so much of modern life. Another
70

aspect of the theme of solitude is Romero's view of the victim in society, the individual who suffers abuse and is misunderstood in a cruel, or at best indifferent world. Each one of the twenty-one stories deals in some way with death. A general classification of the stories, however, would divide them into two groups: those which analyze and reflect on the nature of death itself, and those which portray man as a victim of society. In the stories which fall into the second category, either death or the supernatural serve to strengthen Romero's message.

The first group would include "En la orilla del tiempo" ("At the Edge of Time"), "El forastero" ("The Stranger"), "Esta extraña pared blanca" ("The Strange White Wall"), "La campana de Resurrección" ("The Resurrection Bell"), "El hombre del saco" ("The Man with the Sack"), "El último crimen" ("The Last Crime"), "Testimonio" ("Testimonio"), "El país extranjero" ("Foreign Land"), "La puerta cerrada" ("The Closed Door"), "La carta" ("The Letter"), "Aniversario" ("Anniversary"), "El mar" ("The Sea"), and "El viudo" ("The Widower"). These stories may be further categorized by the narrative viewpoint employed in each one. In eight stories the world is viewed by a "dead" protagonist, who either exists in the "other" world or, as a spirit, visits the place where he lived his mortal life. The other stories deal with the subject of death and life beyond death, but from the perspective of the "living." The narrative point of view which predominates in both categories is either direct interior monologue or indirect interior monologue, an attempt by Romero to allow for the uninhibited expression of ideas and sensations. In all the stories listed above, emphasis is given to the timelessness and solitude of death. Characters are essentially alone and often confused, without a clear concept of time and space. Instead of offering a new life of joy and happiness, or at least a release from the problems of life, death seems only to accentuate the sense of loneliness and isolation which for Romero is characteristic of modern society.

The short stories which involve a "dead" protagonist are particularly effective in emphasizing the timelessness and alienation of the world "beyond." In "Resurrection Bell" ("Campana de Resurrección), the narrator-protagonist lies underground in utter loneliness. Although it is apparent that he is dead, the man is unaware as to why and how long he remains separated from the living. Time has no meaning for him now except in the sense that his "existence" as a dead man appears eternal. He therefore longs for salvation, which is symbolized by the bell of the town's churchtower, and which promises to free him from his corporeal existence in the grave. The Christian overtones of the story are evident as the man awaits the resurrection of his spirit by means of God's grace. "Foreign Land" ("El país extranjero") narrates the recollections of a woman who finds herself somewhere between the world of the living and the dead. Her disorientation and extreme loneliness in this dreamlike state are highlighted by memories of the automobile accident in which she died and by her consideration of arches and a bridge which seemingly offer her a way to the "other" world. In "Anniversary" ("Aniversario") a young man, dead for five years, reveals his isolation from his family as he watches them now dine together. Added to the pain caused by the separation experienced by the man is his observation that the family remains virtually the same as it was five years before. His survivors have failed to take advantage of the opportunities for growth and change in the life which he has been denied. In similar fashion to "The Anniversary," in "The Widower" ("El viudo") a woman sympathetically observes her widowed husband and endures the pain and anguish of not being able to care for him any longer. The loneliness and boredom which he experiences are felt even more acutely by his dead wife.

These narratives which contemplate death from the viewpoint of the living either stress unusual or inexplicable events, or see death in symbolic or allegorical terms. "The Stranger" ("El forastero") relates the appearance of a raggedly dressed man who visits a businessman at his greatest moment of fulfillment and pleasure. The stranger is death itself and is recognized as such by the mortal, who follows the apparition to his own inevitable destruction. The "stranger" is often ignored, but is always present, becoming more "dangerous" or bothersome to the businessman (everyman) in his advancing years. The personification of death in the story as a rough, almost uncouth man underscores the negative and relentless character of time: there are always projects unfinished and dreams unfulfilled when the "stranger" calls. The mailman in "The Letter" ("La carta") is death's messenger who must deliver "the letter" to an unsuspecting housewife. In this story, the reader is unsure what the letter contains, but it is fair to assume that it reveals her husband's, or possibly her own, death. Tension is created between references to life, as revealed in the conversation of the woman with her friend, and death. The duty of the mailman to deliver the letter highlights the inevitability and urgency of the message he bears. Foreshadowing of the tragic news is provided by the stillness of the treadmill—Romero's favorite metaphor of life and human activity—thus suggesting to the woman the nature of the letter she is to receive.

In "The Man with the Sack" ("El hombre del saco"), an old man carries his memories (life) in a sack. When he loses them, he dies. Death, as depicted in this story, deprives man forever of memory, and forces him to exist eternally without a past or a future. Ironically, the old man gains respect and appreciation only from those who observe him travel to the cemetery and his own grave. Never during his lifetime was he even noticed. "Testimony" ("Testimonio") and "The Last Crime" ("El último crimen") depict the mysterious life beyond death. The former relates the experience of a boy, now an adult, who heard the night watchman cry out for the souls of the dead several hours after the watchman was killed by thieves. In "The Last Crime" no one is sure whether a boy commits suicide to join his father in another "City" (one in which only those who are released from this world by death may reside), or whether he is somehow murdered by his dead father's ghost. That would be the "final crime," for his father had committed murder before and was executed the morning before the boy's death.

As we have said, the idea that man is a victim of his society is expressed in a second group of stories which includes "Este que dicen juicio . . ." ("They Call This Judgment"), "Don Plural Cualquiera" ("Mr. Plural Anyone"), "Ha pasado una sombra" ("A Shadow Passed By"), "Los dos mendigos" ("The Two Beggars"), "El muerto que no era" ("The Dead Man Who Wasn't"), "La corona de mariposas" ("The Crown of Butterflies"), "La calle de los niños" ("Children's Street"), and "Los ecos" ("Echoes"). For instance, "The Two Beggars" describes two men who, seen as a composite figure, represent Christ. Rejected and vilified by society, they are innocent victims of the most violent and cruel aspects of human nature.[2] The old man in "The Crown of Butterflies" is the victim of the unjust stratification of the rich and the poor, the bosses and the workers, and has died while performing a good deed for a friend, but no one knows how pure and good he was. Many friends and relatives, however, were repulsed by his poverty and simplicity. At the wake his boss hypocritically pays his respects without regard for the saintly humility and generosity of his employee. Only the old man's wife and dog—his faithful companions—and an innocent child perceive the butterflies which God has placed above the dead man's head. Those who are more concerned with material things are not prepared to accept and experience God's presence, nor are they able to recognize the man's true worth. "The Dead Man Who Wasn't" recounts the vicious murder of a man by his enemy. The day after the crime the assassin learns that he killed the wrong man in a meaningless murder. Anguished by his own stupid error, the assassin suffers a heart attack and dies. "The Dead Man Who Wasn't" emphasizes the theme of man as "victim" of fate or chance, and implies a sense of poetic justice as the criminal suffers the consequences of his own inhumanity.

The stories of *Shadows from Beyond* reveal a concern for fundamental individual problems (death, loneliness, alienation) and social maladies (injustice, violence, poverty). The underlying theme of the continuation of human conflicts pervades virtually the entire collection. In "Echoes" two parallel accounts of an imminent birth (the case of Concha and her husband's grandmother) suggest that Concha may die in childbirth just as the other mother did. Everyone senses and fears the presence of death in Concha's reenactment of the previous event. The story ends before it is resolved, and thus as we anticipate the birth of Concha's child we suspect her untimely death as well. "Children's Street," a story of searching for a street of the past, emphasizes the loneliness of the quest for the meaning of life. It is not clear whether the searcher is dead or alive. Nor do we know if the "street" still exists, or even if it ever did. What is certain is that one cannot relive the past. "Children's Street" is similar to "This Strange White Wall" in that the story involves the conscious evaluation by a dead man of his life, a justification of his existence prior to God's final judgment. Contemplation of the wall leads the dead man to find meaning and approval in the absence of social and material measures of status and personal worth. "Anniversary" and "The Crown of Butterflies" suggest the continuation of the same social patterns generation after generation. Most convincing in this respect are "Mr. Plural Anyone" and "A Shadow Passed By," which depict in detail the repetitiveness of human experience.

The best of the stories of *Shadows from Beyond* are "Mr. Plural Anyone," "They Call This Judgment . . .," "A Shadow Passed By," and "At the Edge of Time," which successfully express the vital concerns characterizing the collection as a whole. Each will be studied in greater detail in the following sections.

II   *"Mr. Plural Anyone"*

In this short story, the life of a man is recalled in a somewhat impersonal manner that tends to lend it a generic dimension. "Mr.

Plural Anyone" is the mental review that a man makes of his life after it has ended. Seen from the perspective of the other world, specific events of earthly existence lose their immediacy; they seem remote.[3] As this man recollects his experiences on earth, he becomes thoughtful and uncovers their deeper meaning, a meaning that up to then had escaped him. In this fashion, for example, he realizes after his death how far from the truth were the words of his political leader (pp. 18–19). The greater understanding of life experienced by the narrator and the impersonal nature in which everything is presented are due, to a large extent, to the generic objectives of the story. When the protagonist recalls his life, he is re-creating a distant event. As he remembers the past, he visualizes the similarities between his life and that of others about him who will follow him to the grave. The very title of the story is an indication of Romero's objectives. The contraposition of the words "plural," "anyone," and "Mr." give the impression of a man whose individual nature (emphasized by the word "Don") is similar to that of his fellow men (the meaning of "plural" and "anyone" support this idea). Mr. Plural Anyone is a man who, without lacking individuality, could easily be confused with any other person. The idea of creating characters who have generic attributes is not new to Romero. In *The Treadmill* and the last chapter of *The Old Voices* there is a similar intention. What is new in "Mr. Plural Anyone" is the mode of presentation, the clear manner in which Romero expresses the idea of the brotherhood of man:

> In his youth he belonged to a political party that was led by a swindler, a somewhat common demagogue, [a man] who didn't even take much trouble to hide the obvious trickery of his deeds. Political triumphs inflamed him, and he thought of himself as "the majority" and the governing class. In his nation, only a third of the citizens were registered, and even though some dead individuals voted, many of the living did not. (p. 18)
> The people—others, many and even a "new him," similar to him—keep on advancing through the subterranean galleries, obeying the commanding arrows, standing on the platform. . . . (p. 50)
> They keep on arriving at the elevators and going up to face their work unhappily. They keep on recounting to one another anecdotes which are stale from so much use, and jokes that make one force a smile. (pp. 51–52)

From these examples it is obvious that someone is describing personal experiences with great detachment as if his deeds were done by others as well. While in the first example the speaker tells us of his youth, in the second he associates with others who behave as he does.

Even more: the second example mentions "a new him," a new entity who has implicitly retraced the narrator's footsteps as the latter follows the path common to humanity. The reference to the "new him" is logical if we remember that what we are reading originates in a dead man, someone capable of observing life objectively, someone with the ability to identify its repetitions (expressions like "keep on arriving" and "keep on recounting" in the third quotation validate our conclusion). Perhaps it is in the following example that the similarities in life are brought out with greatest intensity:

> They were crossing with the others—with themselves—, they fought against the current like salmon. No one remembered where he was going; in darkness guided only by a primordial instinct . . . , they perceived by intuition that they had to go, that they were forced to move fast. (p. 10)

From the man's point of view, life is a recurring cycle. From the perception of man as a brother to his fellow beings emanate some basic characteristics of humanity: solitude, personal emptiness, a desire to escape oppressive forces. As viewed by the narrator, solitude is a constant in life because of the lack of communication between human beings:

> And the solitude was at first a sharp pain and afterwards a discomfort. Until, and after a few minutes had gone by, he realized that he had been always alone, regardless of his sexual encounters. . . . (p. 15)
> He does not march alone—it never appears this way—, for other people walk by him but without communicating, without solidarity, hostile, self-absorbed. (p. 9)

The perpetual presence of solitude is a poignant reminder of the emptiness of human existence—man's lack of purpose—and encourages him to evade his reality, taking refuge, for instance, in the world of the movies.

> One can hear the typewriters and the adding machines, someone goes by, at any moment a boss may issue a reprimand, a slamming door is heard . . . papers and numbers pass before his eyes. The afternoon or the morning of today, or of yesterday, or of a year from now waste away in a useless, boring fashion. One hundred thirty men, one hundred thirty thousand, one hundred thirty million men, or—as he would have thought—one hundred twenty-nine million, nine hundred ninety-nine thousand and one more. . . . (p. 26)
> Winters are long and outside it is cold. Here they are covered, solitude

against solitude, failure against failure, disillusion against disillusion, and they form a group, with similar stories. (p. 27)

It was necessary—it is Saturday and more people attend—to wait in line for more than a quarter of an hour, and it was cold, or hot, or rainy. That is why they now feel pleasure—sitting and trusting that there will be a few pleasant hours. They are in a beautiful garden through which they advance toward an elegant mansion, 2,000 eyes, 1,000 excited respirations. (p. 34)

III   *"They Call This Judgment . . ."*

With this short story Luis Romero focuses once again on an event from the beyond, that final judgment which man is told throughout his life he will face after his death. "They Call This Judgment . . ." is a type of speculation concerning the true nature of justice. Can man be certain of the characteristics of his final trial? Is our conception of good and evil in tune with the beliefs held by those who will evaluate our lives? These are the questions that "They Call This Judgment . . ." places before us.

The protagonist of the story, the accused, finds himself in an absurd trial attempting to justify his life. He is accused, among other things, of having one long, dirty fingernail. The nonsensical nature of the accusation and the way everyone reacts to him leave the character disoriented.

He had been dressed in a gown designed for students and with grotesque drawings that deeply humiliated him. Also, the public laughed openly at any comment made by the accuser, and what was worse, they laughed at his [the accused's] timid excuses. He felt alone, and had it not been because he had to concentrate his attention on his defense, he would have cried. At the moment, the prosecuting attorney, dressed in a formal coat and with his head completely shaven, was pointing at him with anger: "and that miserable man, gentlemen, whose name I do not pronounce out of respect for Your Honesties, that great rascal, has had the audacity to leave his left little fingernail long and dirty for more than twenty years." (p. 107)

The disorientation of man before his final judgment, as he attempts to understand and evaluate his life, is approached by Luis Romero in a more realistic fashion in another story in this collection, "Esta extraña pared blanca" ("This Strange White Wall"). Two things clearly differentiate the two stories.[4] First, in "This Strange White Wall," man is asked to review his past and separate the good from the evil. On doing this, he realizes that there are no clear-cut answers. In

"They Call This Judgment . . ." man's disorientation results not so much from his inability to identify the good and evil in his past as from the fact that those surrounding him appear to have values quite different from his own. Also, and contrasting with "This Strange White Wall," in "They Call This Judgment . . ." man finds himself under attack, accused of crimes he cannot understand. The second major difference between the two stories lies in the environment depicted in them. As we have stated, the prevailing atmosphere in "This Strange White Wall" is realistic, normal, and logical. The other story, as seen in the example quoted from page 107, takes place in an absurd world, a cosmos where man is accused of such absurd deeds as having a long dirty nail and other crimes. The specificity of the complaint strengthens the absurdity of the accusation. In this story everything is grotesque (for instance the dress of the accused, the hair and attire of the prosecutor, and his rhetorical speech to the judges).

Through the use of the absurd, "They Call This Judgment . . ." emphasizes that it is foolish to become obsessed with the thought of what will be expected of us during our final judgment. We are unaware of the principles which will govern that judgment, and we cannot conceive what it will be like, for it is alien to our usual perceptions. The truth of this last assertion is documented by the trial presented in the story. To the accused, as to the reader, it is illogical for the "Poderoso Preboste" to begin a speech by saying "respectable and respected public, Mr. Accused, Lady Chairs . . ." (p. 115).[5]

It should be noted that Luis Romero is not rejecting or, for that matter, affirming the existence of a final judgment. His interest in this story lies in the fact that at times man does things not because he believes in them but because he wishes to comply with what he feels will be expected of him during the final judgment. This type of behavior is what is criticized in "They Call This Judgment . . ." for man may never know what is to be expected of him.

As this short story is read, it should be realized that in part what Romero is presenting is the human tendency to believe the unbelievable, to try to comprehend the incomprehensible. Man does this because he needs to see purpose in life, he requires hope regardless of the negative horizons surrounding him. Thus, after hearing the illogical (illogical to the accused and to the reader) statements of his accusers, the man refuses to change his convictions and still believes that he will receive justice at the hands of those attacking him: "For ten minutes, mute, afraid, dispirited, the accused remained seated on the bench. He did not understand anything; he was sure, however, that justice would be done in his case." (p. 115)

IV "*A Shadow Passed By*"

"A Shadow Passed By" is representative of *Shadows from Beyond* because of its use of the supernatural. This story, the most extensive in the collection, is superior in quality to many of the shorter pieces in *Shadows from Beyond*[6] because of its thematic elaboration and structural complexity. The dominant perspective in "A Shadow Passed By" is that of a dead man who is being taken to the cemetery. As his burial party advances through the streets, he sees a world that has already forgotten him and that continues with its activities. As the dead man views his life the reader concludes that at best he was a mere shadow when alive. "A Shadow Passed By" is divided into three sections. The procession preceding the burial constitutes the first part (pp. 177–224). It is here that the dead man reviews his life as his body is being transported to the cemetery. Each place or person "seen" by the dead man allows him to recall specific events in his past. Thus, we have a fragmentary portrait of a man's life that, as far as structure is concerned, reminds us of *The Treadmill*. In the first section, the dead man begins to understand the solitude of his life and how he has been forgotten by everyone. The protagonist's wishes to remain alive a while longer give a degree of cohesiveness to the many fragments which make up the first section:

If they were to allow him to speak, to say hello to these people, to pay the bill. . . . (p. 177)
And this film that they announced today, he would like to see as well. They should stop, please! He does not wish to go ahead. At least a few hours. (p. 179)[7]

In the second section, the dead man is already buried (pp. 224–35). The continuous process of life is emphasized here in a similar fashion to that of *The Old Voices* and another short story in this collection, "Echoes." The people seen by the dead man as he went to the cemetery now are observed in their daily tasks. In this section the narrator is not only telling us that life continues, but in addition he perceives life as a repetition, just as in *The Old Voices*. Since Eduardo, the dead man's assistant, is seen to share some of the traits which his mentor had as a youth, it is obvious that Eduardo's relationship to the dead man is little different from that of the deceased to his former boss, Don Arturo.

The third section (pp. 235–36) is a return to the cemetery. It is here that the dead man fully understands the true meaning of his solitude and sees in God his only hope:

> He cannot see, he does not know, he does not understand. He is alone, more lonely than ever. My God! How long do I have to endure this solitude? Until when? Everything is silent. He waits only for Your word. (p. 236)

As visualized in "A Shadow Passed By," death is not rest. In this condition the dead suffer greater solitude than the living, for after death all voices and memories cease to exist (pp. 235–36).

The principle techniques used to express the dead man's feelings in the story are the indirect interior monologue along with first-person statements:

> He should enter the school right now to say good-bye to all. But, if they were to ask him for the lesson, "I did not know that this lesson was due today; I have come only to say good-bye . . .!" (p. 184)

Also, and part of the indirect interior monologue, there is the ability of the dead man to imagine what the people he observes are thinking. The use of imagination allows for the expansion of the horizons of the story and contributes to the supernatural atmosphere that prevails throughout the narrative:

> They are used to seeing death pass before their doors. At times, it has stopped here; they are dressed in black. "A rich man"—they think—, because the concept of wealth is relative. . . . (p. 218)

V *"At the Edge of Time"*

From a technical point of view, the most innovative of Romero's stories is "At the Edge of Time." Its theme is the timelessness of death. All that was restricted by time before death is now freed from its boundaries. This idea is developed in the story through the eyes of a dead man (Pedro) who, upon recalling and evaluating his life and experiences, cannot distinguish between the past, the present, and

the future. He is, as the title indicates, at the banks of the river which
is time.

> I don't know if I was, am or will be. I remember vaguely that at one time I
> was sure that I was. But was, will be or am no longer are words with any value
> in my mind. Something happened to bring me back to this place in time:
> something that we simply call death. (p. 237)
> Once again time has lost its meaning, and I find myself here, far from the
> ticking [of clocks]. What happened? What did all this mean? Mom, dad,
> teachers, the black woman, my aunt, the lawyer, my wife. . . . Where?
> When? Everything seemed to have such a sure, precise rhythm—yesterday,
> today, tomorrow—. What could have happened? I don't know if I was, am or
> will be. (p. 250)

No longer do the limitations of chronological time have any bearing
on his existence. This loss of the notion of chronological time is
illustrated effectively in another example from the story:

> Now, *thinking* and *tying* up loose ends, I *realized* what *has happened* with
> my mother. Until today I *will not understand* it clearly. And I set myself a
> goal to last my whole life. My mother *would not exist* for me only if she *had
> died*, but something even more radical: I *will not have* a mother; I never
> *thought* about her again. I *learned* by accident that my mother *will run* off with
> my cousin; it *is* a horrible shock to me; but I *decided* to overcome it and I
> *overcome* it. (p. 247, our italics)

In this brief paragraph there are varying combinations of verb forms,
each indicating a different moment in time: gerund, present, pre-
terit, present perfect, and future indicative; conditional; and past-
perfect subjunctive. Despite such a mixture of tenses, however, the
paragraph is not incoherent. More importantly, the reader is not
perplexed by the changes in tense, and, instead, he is "surrounded"
by time and thus accepts without protest the lack of chronological
order.
    Another factor in the destruction of chronological time in the story
is the continual movement of Pedro's thoughts from his death to
childhood, returning once again to the "present" in which the
protagonist-narrator repeats the opening phrase of the story: "I don't
know if I was, am, or will be." In effect, in "At the Edge of Time,"
Luis Romero succeeds in destroying the traditional concept of
chronological time and going beyond its boundaries.

VI   Tudá

A second collection of short stories, *Tudá*,[8] was published in 1957. It is concerned with an historical event: the activities of the Spanish Blue Division on the Russian front during World War II. Romero's primary objective in *Tudá* is to provide a realistic view of the war as experienced by the soldiers. Thus, in our study it is difficult for us to approach each story individually, for all of them are basically part of a more complex organism.[9] Consequently, and to do justice to stories must perforce fail to capture the deeper meaning they have as past of a more complex organism.[9] Consequently, and to do justice to *Tudá*, we have placed emphasis on that view of the cosmos which is provided by the stories as a group. As we do this we shall document our position with a brief statement concerning each narrative.

To achieve his thematic objective, Romero includes ten stories in the volume. The first six are concerned with individual characters as they face specific problems. In this fashion, "La cruz de madera" ("The Wooden Cross") presents a father who had neglected his son during his lifetime. Burdened with guilt, the man seeks to establish his blood ties with his illegitimate son by replacing the cross that lies on his son's grave in the battlefield with one that bears his real last name (that of the negligent father). "La pequeña paz" ("The Small Peace") presents two friends, Jaime and Manolo, enjoying a moment of calm during the war. The peace referred to in the title of the story concerns the relationship of these men, for in Spain they could not be friends because they were separated by the distance between their social classes.

"El recuerdo amargo" ("The Bitter Memory") relates Ricardo's guilt-ridden memory of a friend whom he insulted and who as a result lost his life at the hands of the Russians in a heroic but probably suicidal encounter. "El golpe de mano" ("The Attack") describes the preparation and realization of a limited military operation against the Russians. Most of the story concerns the anticipation of the attack, an event that transpires in only a few moments compared to the length of the wait. "Krasnybor" is somewhat similar to "The Bitter Memory" in that the narrator is recalling how his betrayal of a friend, Angel, probably led to Angel's death. In both stories the narrators are motivated by guilt as they explore their past. Finally, "La partida" ("The Card Game") captures the emptiness of daily life in an artillery company. The card game becomes an escape to the men as they wait to attack or to be attacked.

The final four stories may be seen as the second part of *Tudá*. Each is a soliloquy which treats important aspects of the war on the Russian front through the eyes of the foot soldier, the sentinel, the wounded combat victim, and the repatriates. In each case Romero utilizes the circumstances of the individual to illustrate the many problems and concerns of the Spanish soldiers. The central theme is therefore that of the effects of war on man in general and on the men of the Blue Division in particular. An examination of the four studies reveals the validity of our conclusions.

In "Soliloquio del soldado en marcha" ("Foot Soldier's Soliloquy") we witness the private thoughts of a man who volunteered to join the Spanish Blue Division and is now forced to walk the lonely highways of Russia without really knowing his destination or if he will survive the battles that await him. The tempo of the story is captured in its first paragraph as this soldier views the surrounding reality as a never-ending, slow, and boring process:

> To look at one's feet inevitably provokes motion sickness; it is not that the movement is fast—the whole column is moving slowly, with uniformity—but the movement repeats itself endlessly. . . . One may seek distraction in counting; one, two, one, two, one, two, or in adopting another rhythm: one, two, three, one, two, three, but even this, in the long run, becomes boring. How many steps will be taken during this day? Thousands, perhaps, thousands of thousands. (p. 169)

The foot soldier wanders mentally from one event to another without regard to chronology or content. Thus, after thinking of the march on the Stalin Highway, he considers the abuses of the Communists during the Russian Revolution and, as a result, how the Spanish Communists behaved similarly to their Russian counterparts during the Civil War. Among the thoughts crossing the foot soldier's mind are the flatness of the Russian landscape, how the Blue Division will eliminate the oppressive *caciques* when it returns to Spain, doubts confronting the soldiers concerning the worthiness of their cause and the true intentions of the Germans (their treatment of the Jews and Poles strengthen the soldier's reservations), physical pains suffered by the infantryman as he is forced to walk constantly, etc.

Even though they are fragmentary in nature, the association of ideas having little in common is not too forceful, for the foot soldier is simply allowing his mind to flow as one thought carries within itself the seeds of the next. A clear example of the process of association appears on pages 172–73, when the soldier considers a foot wound as positive because it will allow him to go to the hospital and avoid the daily discomforts of his life as an infantryman. Among the hospital's advantages identified by the soldier are the beautiful nurses, whose presence suggests other women in his past. Undoubtedly the mental associations we have referred to in our analysis result from the dominant narrative technique used in the soliloquies, the interior monologue, a means of expression that is used here to permit the character to transcend the hostile world surrounding him: "If I had received a letter from home this would please me, because then, with what they say, one has more things to think about. I have discovered that if during the long walks you are thinking about something in particular, the kilometers seem shorter because time goes by unnoticed" (p. 183). Thinking—the interior monologue—becomes then a deliberate means of escaping one's negative environment.

Although throughout "Foot Soldier's Soliloquy" there is a tendency to present the fragmentary mental reality of a man, this does not prevent a cohesive view of the cosmos from emerging. Thus, the soldier of the soliloquy becomes at once a sensitive human being to the Russian prisoners (he feels attracted to them, p. 107) and an adversary who experiences great hostility toward the Russians when viewed in their totality and as enemies (as when he imagines his wife marrying a Russian, p. 186). The juxtaposition of compassion and hate gives life to our visualization of the foot soldier as a human being and contributes to our understanding of his complex personality and generic attributes. As portrayed in the soliloquy we are studying, the foot soldier thinks of himself as a crusader, a man defending social justice (pp. 172, 178, 181) by fighting alongside the Germans (the latter representing order and civilization). As the foot soldier contemplates the importance of his deeds, he observes traits in his German allies that disturb his conscience (as with the German abuse of the Jewish people, p. 179). When confronted with a contradictory world, the foot soldier becomes disoriented and frustrated because he finds himself without clear guidance: "in reality we do not know what will take place and if we have come here to risk our lives and to be the protagonists of war, we should at least know where the world is heading" (p. 177).

It should be noted that the foot soldier lacks a proper name in the short story. In omitting this Luis Romero is placing emphasis not only on the personal reality of one man, but in his similarities with his counterparts on the Stalin Highway. On this last point, the division of the short story is indeed significant. From page 169 to page 204 the dominant perspective is that of a man whose name remains unknown to us. On page 204, the last paragraph of the story is typographically separated from its main body with three stars. The narrator here is not the foot soldier; rather, it is an impersonal voice describing his place in the column and identifying by name those surrounding the man who narrated the first part of the short fiction. The impersonal narrator establishes common characteristics among the Spanish soldiers. Thus the thoughts of the foot soldier become, implicitly, those of his counterparts in the Blue Division: the tragedy of war is at once that of one man and of all men.

The remaining three soliloquies are very similar in form and content to the one we just studied. In this fashion, all three make use of mental processes to express the hardships of the soldier: his fears, boredom, physical deprivation, idealism, memories, and hopes. Each story, however, adds new characteristics to the soldier's reality.

In "Soliloquio del centinela" ("Sentinel's Soliloquy"), for instance, a soldier meditates during his hour of guard duty. Prominent among his many thoughts is his contradictory attitude toward the war in which he is fighting. At times he has decided to risk everything—and to suffer, if necessary—for his cause, while on other occasions he wishes to be wounded and as a result to leave the battlefield and escape the hostile surroundings. Within the sentinel, courage and fear coexist simultaneously. These emotions lead him to imagine events that at once vivify the horrors attributed to the Russians and his personal salvation. An example of what we are discussing appears when the sentinel imagines how he is wounded and taken prisoner by the feared Russians but is spared dying before a firing squad by a former girl friend, Marisa Rubio, whose Communist ideology allowed her to exert great influence over her comrades (pp. 214–15). By fantasizing, the sentinel is then adding dramatic intensity to his situation, thereby evading—as was the case with the foot soldier—the unglamorous and brutal reality of the battlefield.

The "Soliloquio del herido" ("Wounded Combat Victim's Soliloquy") expresses the uncertainty of a man fallen victim to enemy fire, a man who comes to wonder whether he is dead or alive (p. 237). From the battlefield, this story takes us to the reality of the wounded, a world feared and, at times, desired by the soldiers. In his convalescence, the wounded man recalls his past, the time spent with his loved ones, and his guilt in knowing that he survived his brothers after they were taken prisoners by the hated Communists during the

Spanish Civil War. The reference to Spain's armed conflict reminds the reader that the Blue Division's participation in World War II resulted from another military confrontation, one that still exerted influence upon many Spaniards.

The last story in *Tudá*, "Soliloquio de los repatriados" ("Repatriates' Soliloquy"), concerns itself with the speculations and memories of a soldier about to return to Spain after his tour of duty on the Russian front. Among the concerns of this man is his unhappiness (perhaps even guilt), for he is returning to his homeland knowing that his comrades will stay behind fighting an endless battle (p. 274). As the repatriate thinks of his future return, he remembers his past at the Russian front and imagines the reception he will receive in Spain.

Of significance is how the title of the collection of short stories relates to the special aspects of Spain's armed intervention on foreign soil. *Tudá*, in Russian, and the subtitle *Allá (There)* in Spanish, refer to a military conflict far away from Spain, in this case, on the Russian front.[10] The uniqueness of this conflict, in contrast to the Spanish Civil War, is manifest in the following reflection by one of the soldiers:

> But the Spanish war was another matter; something fatal and unavoidable, in which everyone became involved. It was a tragic risk, in which all were participants, especially those in actual combat, and which troubled every family. Now it's different: he has sought his own personal destiny, shared with only a few thousand young men from all over Spain. (p. 89)

In a similar way, the idea of distance prevails among the soldiers who recall friends and events "back there," in Spain. The juxtaposition of simultaneous events, as envisioned in the mind of one of the men, is effective in expressing the sense of separation and loneliness experienced by the troops, and the lack of comprehension on the part of countrymen and friends "there" (Spain) regarding the miserable conditions which the soldiers endure. Diego Rodríguez notices the time of day and immediately thinks of the easy life his friends are enjoying in Madrid (pp. 79–80). The wounded soldier longs to be with his wife (especially as his condition worsens) and begins to imagine himself at home with his family (pp. 242 and 245). One example from the book reveals not only the awareness of separation made implicit by simultaneous but distant events, but the most difficult conditions of wartime:

It must be three o'clock already. He doesn't want to look at his watch; it infuriates him to pass the time constantly looking at the clock. Menchu will explain to whomever will listen that her fiancé was brave, certainly she'll say that "he died like a hero"; but she must now know that he is here now, filled with anxieties, and that the cold, the smoke and lice bother him . . . and that instead of spending his last hours thinking about transcendental matters, his mind is simply wandering, letting itself be rocked by the ebb and flow of ideas, trusting that the minutes will pass by quickly and, pushed by them, the hours; let the Captain arrive to give them the latest orders. (pp. 98–99)

Greater than the physical hardships which the soldier must withstand is the tension produced by the constant atmosphere of danger and the resultant fear that death may occur at any time. The soldiers' preoccupation with death is heightened by the suggestion that their ultimate sacrifice is practically devoid of significance. Instead of a war of great ideals and principles it is reduced to a contest between a few Russians, Germans, and Spaniards who as individuals do not hate one another, but who are nevertheless locked in combat:[11]

In the final analysis, so much war and destruction so that a Russian lies on one side of the road, and two Germans on the other, and who knows if before a month is out there will be a cross, about this large, with my name [on it] and there I will be rotting underneath; it's not that I'm panicky about that happening, but it does make me a bit sad. . . . (pp. 195–96)

Ultimately, the uncertainty concerning life or death in war heightens the soldier's sense of solitude and helplessness:

Once again there is silence, a heavy silence, which seems to have sat down among us. To speak is beautiful; to speak with another man. To speak when there's lots to say and at the same time one doesn't know what to say. To speak when one suspects that perhaps it's for the last time. . . . Men should talk more among themselves, get to know each other better. After all, what does one person know about all the rest? And everyone else about each one? We go through the world elbow to elbow, hurting or loving each other, but without each other. (p. 97)

To present effectively the influence of war on the individual, Romero utilizes variations of the first-person narrative viewpoint with some success, allowing the reader to participate in the hardships of the soldiers. The use of indirect interior monologue (for example,

p. 101) and direct interior monologue, plural and singular (pp. 115 and 117, and the soliloquies), contributes to the expression of personal memories and reflections. Dialogue (p. 143) draws the reader immediately into the conversation and the reality of war. These techniques are effective in the stories. However, Romero employs interior monologue in the soliloquies with such little variety and imagination that they are monotonous to the reader ("Soliloquio del centinela" ["Sentinel's Soliloquy"], for example). Perhaps some tediousness results from Romero's emphasizing the routine of daily life on the front. Although the simplistic conversation of "La partida" ("The Card Game") conveys the image of the "hard shell" that protects the soldiers from the constant threat of death, it also lacks any sense of profundity and appears to continue endlessly without meaningful variation.

VII   Christmas Eve

In his novel *Christmas Eve*[12] Luis Romero reinterprets the Christmas story using a large city and its working-class inhabitants as the setting for the arrival of Joseph and Mary from a poor and remote village. Unable to locate even the cheapest accommodations for the night, the couple is forced to return to the train station and seek refuge in an abandoned cattle car. It is in that improvised manger that their son is born.

Although the two peasants are completely unknown and virtually lost in the city, strangers appear as if miraculously to render assistance to them. An old woman hears the muffled cries of Mary and is at once at her side as midwife and friend. "Grandfather Angel," as he is called by the residents of the railyard slum, dedicates all his energies during the night to announcing the news of the birth of the Son of God and to obtaining food and clothing for the new arrivals. A special overtime shift of workers also becomes involved in Angel's efforts. The engineer decides to defy company rules and heat the couple's car with the stove of the locomotive. Laborers donate money and food and Angel is able to induce some vagabonds to contribute to the cause. During the course of the evening, therefore, a host of common folk respond, all at some personal sacrifice, to the needs of Joseph, Mary, and the newborn child. Their despair and solitude are transformed in one evening into hope and a sense of community.

The parallel histories of Christ and the peasants' child are employed to emphasize the coexistence of good and evil in the world.

However, despite the potential of the Christmas story as a means to convey this theme (a constant in the novels of Romero), its elaboration is marred by oversimplification and too obvious symbolism.[13] Good is exemplified by Angel, the woman, the engineer, and others whose sacrifices are well received by the young couple. Joseph expresses his belief that divine will was at work during the events of the evening: " 'We'll be fine until tomorrow. We're fine; everything is over now. It was quite a scare at first, but an old woman has helped us, we don't even know her name, and I don't see her around here now. One can see that it was God's will that things turned out as they have' " (p. 186).[14]

Evil, on the other hand, is evident from the numerous examples of indifference on the part of society and individuals to the suffering of one's neighbor. Those who own property or have other possessions exploit the poor and uneducated, as in the case of the owners of the railroad line and their employees.[15] In another instance, a couple whose livelihood depends on a modest income from eggs and poultry attempts to shoot two thieves the wife observes running from their premises. But the greatest disparity between good and evil exists because people fail to recognize the qualities of those who are virtuous. The vagabonds ridicule Grandfather Angel; the fireman (who admits to having beaten his wife on their wedding night) angrily snaps at his companion when the engineer risks his job to help the present couple; and local citizens ignore Joseph and Mary even when they see the two before them: "They all share the joy of the moment, the passing happiness of this night, in which the cold somehow seems less cold than it is, misery, less miserable, and solitude, less solitary. Because of the mild intoxication which they all share, no one notices Joseph and Mary walk among them" (p. 65). The realities of everyday experience are ignored by the passerby because of the celebration of Christmas. Even though they do so unintentionally, their failure to aid the good couple suggests the sin of omission which characterizes modern society.[16]

The idea of the coexistence of good and evil is developed in *Christmas Eve* by means of the presentation of simultaneous events. As in other novels, particularly *The Others* and *The Current*, consecutive chapters deal at times with the same event, thus creating a sense of density around each one and providing different, sometimes opposite, perspectives of separate characters. The reader, then, perceives that at the same time one man may discuss his conquests of women, and another, his family obligations; one may

laugh about the birth of a child in a cattle car, and another see the
event as sacred. It is possible, therefore, that while evil actions are
committed, these are offset by the goodwill of others.

Each of the chapters of *Christmas Eve* focuses upon a particular
circumstance or view of events as interpreted by a given character.
The scope of vision of each chapter is achieved by manipulating point
of view in three ways: through dialogue (p. 22), indirect interior
monologue (pp. 20, 21, 95), and the commentary of an omniscient
narrator who reflects upon the experience of a character. The
following description illustrates this final technique (the italics are
ours): "They look at each other; the word hotel frightens and
disillusions them. Since the entrance is deserted and no one is visible
through the glass, Mary risks a peek through the window. *It's a
decrepit hotel, rank, one that grew old in those worn-out side streets.*
Two dwarf palms, each in a matching flowerpot, flank the entrance"
(p. 58). She is the one who notices the deterioration of the building,
but it is the narrator who places what Mary sees in perspective with
the location of the hotel.

On another occasion the author momentarily abandons his omniscience to speculate on the motives of streetcar passengers who enjoy
making fun of Joseph and Mary:

The streetcar approaches, packed with men and women who have finished
their day's work. The passengers are squeezed together and crowded next to
the conductor. They've just seen two peasants who are carrying bundles as
they walk between the rails. When the conductor loudly announces his
intention of giving the couple a scare, everyone rejoices. Perhaps in the
darkness they're unable to discern the poverty of [the couple's] clothes, the
painful deformity of their shoes, and the pregnant condition of the woman.
When they're virtually upon them, with one hand on the brake, the
conductor steadily and violently rings the [foot-operated]bell. Everyone
laughs as they see the couple jump with fear to reach the sidewalk. (p. 74)

The narrator suggests that perhaps the passengers act out of ignorance instead of malice.[17]

Christmas Eve never escapes the Manichean simplicity of its
themes and the weariness of redundant description, weakened by
overstatement. Stress in characterization shifts awkwardly from
Joseph and Mary to a series of bland, unconvincing scenes of
exploited workers and inhabitants of the city's slum area. The novel
abruptly ends with a description of Holy Week ceremonies in

Barcelona which have become a tourist attraction, and thus Romero
returns again to the overworked theme of insensitivity to and
distortion by society of the spiritual values symbolized by the faith
which it claims to profess.

VIII   *"The Treadmill of Memories"*

From June 15, 1963, to July 11, 1964, Romero wrote a column in
the Barcelona weekly *Destino* entitled "La noria de los recuerdos"
("The Treadmill of Memories"). In each column Romero narrates
sometime from his past either in first-person singular or plural.[18] At
times the author centers his attention on local customs (as in "Noche
de San Juan" and "La mascletá"), typical places he has visited (for
instance, "Ugíjar," "La dedicatoria," "La Chanca"), or colorful
people he has met ("Los arrabales"). Quite often in these realistic
vignettes so reminiscent of the Spanish *costumbristas* of the
nineteenth century, the past is viewed with nostalgia, as if it had
disappeared or were about to do so (see "El puente del diablo" and
"Comida en el molino").[19] On occasion, Romero recalls circumstances that to him show social injustice and that still provoke in
him moralizing statements (examples appear in "Torremolinos," "Los
grandes hombres," "La Chanca," and "Los monederos falsos").

The title of the column clearly reminds us of Romero's first novel,
The Treadmill. However, in the short narratives of "The Treadmill of
Memories" he is not concerned with the presentation of man as an
individual entity and with his place in the complex machine of
society. In "The Treadmill of Memories" Romero is figuratively using
the term "treadmill" to remind the reader that his vignettes are like
water brought to the surface by the buckets of a chain pump: they are
just a few memories drawn from the deep well of the past.

IX   *Other Short Stories*

The stories included in this section are a sample of the many short
narratives written by Luis Romero and published over the years in
various journals.[20] In most cases they explore themes that appear
elsewhere in Romero's literary production. "La barca" ("The Boat")[21]
is the story of a smuggler who remembers his childhood encounter
with another smuggler. As an adult his role is changed: he is now the
contrabandist who meets a child on a deserted beach. As he describes

his encounter with the young boy, the adult narrator is constantly
aware of having experienced the event before. At first it is just a
sensation, a fuzzy recollection of his childhood. He is prone to
recalling experiences of his youth, for in his childhood ·memories he
finds a sense of well-being and happiness. But now the older man
realizes that *he* is the boy, for he learns that the youth has his name.
He greets the child and kisses him exactly as the smuggler did to him
a generation ago. Thus in "The Boat" life is presented as a continuing
cycle.

"El cumpleaños de Elena" ("Elena's Birthday")[22] and "La playa"
("The Beach")[23] present characters sustaining private dialogues
within themselves. In "Elena's Birthday" it appears that a child
witnesses how his happy sister, Elena, wishes during her birthday
that time will fly so that she may as an adult experience life more fully.
The brother reacts with fear because he seems to know what the
future has in store for Elena. It is not clear how the child can
anticipate Elena's death on the beach. Perhaps the narrator is a man
who remembers the death of his sister and proceeds to associate this
event in his mind with her eleventh birthday. The mystery surrounding the narrator's fears is reminiscent of this emotion as experienced
in *Shadows from Beyond.*

Of particular interest in "Elena's Birthday" is the use of the child's
point of view. Romero is partially successful in presenting reality
through the eyes of a thirteen-year-old boy. Elena's older brother
reveals his envy of César, a first-year law student and friend of the
family. The brother resents the fact that his father treats César as an
adult (he offers him a cigarette), and is repulsed by even imagining
the possibility that César would be Elena's future husband. As their
mother contemplates many children for Elena, the boy is embarras-
sed by the thought of his sister having sexual relations. He imagines
her belly filled with children, and he is not content again until the
topic of conversation changes and Elena is restored in his mind's eye
as an innocent eleven-year-old. Despite success in interpreting
events through the eyes of an adolescent, the ingenuousness of the
child-narrator's point of view is altered because of the incursion of
"grown-up" words and concepts. The use of these terms suggests that
the action of the story is being recalled in the memory of an adult
narrator. Words such as "surreptitiously" (p. 151) and "loquacious"
(p. 154) are hardly standard vocabulary for a thirteen-year-old. Even
more "adult," however, is the preoccupation—almost obsession—

with the passage of time. As he considers the birthday dinner, the boy wishes to prolong the experience and protect it from the inevitable effects of time: "I would like to secure it [the instant], to keep it from merging with amorphous time, in the fatal succession of events. I'm anguished by the fact that everything is condemned to be erased, that nothing from this moment, now so distinct and intense, will remain" (p. 152). And yet this memory will remain, and will preserve the event intact as if it were a photograph in the mind of the narrator: "The birthday dinner continues; I am aware of the perfection of the moment, of the tepid happiness which surrounds and protects us in the intimacy of this family fortress of a birthday without end" (p. 155). The interruption of the narrative action by a dreamlike sequence which describes Elena's drowning further implies an adult narrator. This section, highlighted throughout by the use of italics, records the confusion and anguish which characterize the discovery on the beach of Elena's dead body. Although the crowd tries to keep the brother from seeing his sister, he catches a glimpse of her (actually he sees only her discolored feet). This image has become a permanent vision, the most persistent and nagging memory of the girl he prefers to recall as a charmingly capricious eleven-year-old. By sandwiching the scene of Elena's death between the detached elements of a single recollection (the birthday meal), Romero is able to maintain the dual adult-child view of reality. Seen from the perspective of the boy, Elena's death is but a terrible dream, a future event which stands in ironic contrast to the pleasantness of the present. To an adult narrator, however, the second section of the story has already occurred. The obsession with the passage of time revealed in parts one and three reflects his wish to replace the horrifying memory with a more positive image of his sister.

"The Beach" is the monologue of a man who evaluates his life while standing on the balcony of a hotel owned by a company he controls. Despite his protests to the contrary, he feels guilty for changing the world he enjoyed with a woman during their youth, for replacing spiritual values with material luxuries. Symbolic of the transformation that has occurred within him is his inability to locate in the vast panorama below the simple house in which the couple first settled down. As he claims that now he contributes to society's improvement, the reader realizes that the man is trying to rationalize that his present life is more fulfilling than the one he shared with his beloved. Now he is devoid of human warmth and understanding, having conceded to the past the free-spirited happiness of the love he once knew.

The business tycoon's seemingly indifferent attitude to the sentimental importance of the little house, the plight of the poor, the exploitation of the labor force, and the starving children of Biafra, complements his insistence that the luxurious tourist-hotel complex actually has improved the landscape of the seashore. He argues that such accommodations are "appropriate" for the many foreign tourists and wealthy Spaniards who seek leisure and relaxation at the expense of the common people. And yet, in a brief moment of honest reflection, the businessman abruptly and rather unexpectedly concludes that his company is indeed guilty of destroying the landscape (p. 13). He is unmoved by this realization, however, and promptly dismisses the idea as he contemplates pending business transactions. It is apparent that his many admonitions in defense of his actions ("Don't believe"; "I assure you"; "I swear") are thinly disguised justifications for having lost the freedom and naturalness of his early adulthood. It seems, therefore, that the man is aware of but unable to accept responsibility for his own lack of spiritual and social values. "The Beach," like "Bitter Memory" and "Krasnybor" in *Tudá*, presents the dissatisfaction of a human being with what he has done, his inability to forget, and the corrosive effects of guilt.

The plots of "El hombre justo" ("The Just Man")[24] and "El día en que terminó la guerra" ("The Day the War Ended")[25] deal with events that relate to the Spanish Civil War, a topic that led Romero to write *Three Days in July, Disaster in Cartagena,* and *The End of the War.* "The Just Man" is the narration of how a prisoner, as part of his punishment, is forced to select which of his peers will not die before a firing squad. The young narrator in this story is one of four persons chosen to be saved by that "just man" who is tortured by the responsibility he is forced to assume for the fate of other prisoners. And as survivors, a mother, her child, an old man, and the boy-narrator must forever share some of the guilt experienced by the man who saved them. "The Day the War Ended" serves to emphasize how the horrors of war continue long after its conclusion. An innocent boy who during the war experienced terror, years later commits a murder in order to obtain the wealth that a deserter had stolen and hidden away the day the war ended. Through the tale of the boy who becomes a murderer and the depiction of the avarice that motivated his elders during his youth, Romero presents the Spanish Civil War as an unending event, one that continues to influence many lives.

X *Conclusion*

In this chapter, we have examined three of Luis Romero's books *(Shadows from Beyond, Tudá,* and *Christmas Eve),* a collection of autobiographical vignettes, and five short stories. The writings studied here are of unequal artistic merit. At one end of the spectrum, we find certain narratives in which Romero has shown considerable skill in presenting the generic traits of mankind, in portraying reality as absurd, and in manipulating verb tenses in order to create a feeling of timelessness. We find at the opposite end of the spectrum the use of obvious symbolism in *Christmas Eve.* However, the narratives under consideration in this chapter have many characteristics in common, among which are Romero's constant preoccupation with man, the injustice society forces upon him, and the solitude and emptiness of his existence.

CHAPTER 7

A New Aesthetic Dimension

W INNER of the Planeta Prize for 1963,[1] Romero's *El cacique* (*The Boss*) gives evidence of the author's continuing development as a fiction writer. *The Boss* is his best novel since *The Treadmill,* and although it shows the influence of previous works, it displays important changes in theme and style which are unique in Romero's novelistic production.

Despite the fact that he never appears as a character, the *cacique* (boss) whose death is announced at the novel's outset is the invisible but omnipresent protagonist of *The Boss.* [2] His life and influence manifest themselves as a plethora of characters (no less than ninety-seven) from a rural Spanish town are presented in successive chapters of the novel. All of the characters are affected in some way by the unnamed despot, and among them are some of Romero's most vivid creations. Gregoria and Zacarías, peasants who alone dared to challenge the *cacique* when he claimed some of their land, now openly return to work the fields which lay uncultivated during five years of legal disputes. Doctor Escorihuela, the only physician in the village, worries about a possible challenge to his methods by a more widely recognized professional authority. Don Eloy is the man who has benefited so much as personal lawyer to the boss. Basilia, an attractive young woman, decides to leave town after having been humiliated and dishonored by the powerful landowner. Rosita, a former mistress of the *cacique,* awaits the reading of the will, which she hopes will provide her and her mother with a modest income. The sexton, who immediately after the boss's death hurries to warn "the Stutterer" of impending danger, is ironically the one whose weakness for wine and women allows a group of circus performers to steal the diamond ring from the entombed body of the cacique. Other interesting characters abound: the sons of the *cacique,* the provincial governor, the mayor, the local schoolteacher, and a blind beggar

96

who, despite his public eulogies of the powerful landowner, openly reveals his dislike in private conversation.

During the time between the death and the burial of the boss, the townspeople steadily express a sense of relief, even joy, over his death. Their true feelings of anger, hatred, greed, anxiety, and frustration become evident as their lives unfold before us. Although *The Boss* is clearly a "social" novel, like most of Luis Romero's previous works, it has an ambiguity which is an important factor in its successful construction. Even though signs point to Don Froilán as the successor to the *cacique* the question of the town's future remains undecided. Basilia leaves town, never to be heard from again. No one is sure whether or not "The Stutterer" will return to avenge the violent attack on his home by a mob of townspeople. The theft of the ring, achieved by slicing off one of the cadaver's fingers, takes place with no evidence that the crime will be revealed, and it is most unlikely that the circus performers will be captured.[3] Uncertainty is thus a major force in the novel. It culminates with the *cacique*'s will: no one, save Don Fernando, knows what it contains, nor what effect it will have on the survivors. Thus reality is something rather ambiguous, unclear, to those who try to comprehend the world which surrounds them.[4] With *The Boss*, Romero has given us one of his best novels, for as Gerard Genette has stated, "The whole art of literature consists in turning language (which is a somewhat expeditious means of communicating knowledge and opinion) into a thing of uncertainty and questioning."[5]

I   *Social Injustices*

The most important theme of the novel, as indicated by the title, is that of *caciquismo* (bossism), the pervasive and controlling influence of the *cacique* in virtually all aspects of life in the rural village. The novel presents the vision of a town only recently relieved of the terror and power of its oppressor. His death is the cause of joyful celebration and also of a spontaneous release of emotion which reveals the hate and fear which have been repressed during his lifetime. The boss, whose name is perhaps too odious or terrible to pronounce, becomes the archetypal *cacique* whose presence in rural Spanish communities still has not been erased by the "progress" of contemporary society.

Of course the theme of *caciquismo* refers to basic social injustices, the abuse of power and influence in the everyday lives of the townspeople. In *The Boss* the rich increase their wealth by exploiting the masses who serve them. "Law and order" are the watchwords of the powerful: the feudal landowner, his lawyer, the police, the governor, the business leaders. Of greatest significance, of course, is the concept of order, because laws are either utilized to exploit the poor, or defied by the boss and his followers in the pursuit of wealth and power. On one occasion, instead of yielding to the demands of farm workers for wages which would allow for at least a meager existence for their families, the boss had ordered the destruction of the olive crop rather than concede an additional two *reales* for their day's labor. And despite his death, the townspeople's dreams of justice are subverted by the ambitious and greedy few who immediately ally themselves with Don Froilán, a ruthless and greedy usurer. Returning from the funeral service, townspeople hurry to seek his favor, thus establishing him as the community's new boss: "The mayor, with his colleagues, approaches Don Froilán also. Many of the people surround him, and try to shake his hand or speak to him; he remains solemn, attentive but aloof" (p. 319).

Greed, the primary cause of the social injustices perpetrated by the *cacique* and his ilk, colors the atmosphere of the whole town, reaching individuals outside the realm of the strong and powerful. The focus and object of such greed is the diamond ring which everyone admires as the boss lies in state prior to the funeral. Given the opportunity, practically everyone would like to share the wealth of the despot. Ironically, only the group of outsiders, the itinerant circus performers, are able to realize that dream by robbing the grave.

It seems that the one resource available to the townspeople and nearby farmers to curb the power of the *cacique* is never fully understood. Immediately after news of his death, a group of men decide to storm the home of his "enforcer," unceremoniously nicknamed "The Stutterer." Seeing the ugly mood of the mob, "The Stutterer" chooses to flee for safety. He never returns. But the townspeople fail to recognize the potential strength and influence of their unity, of solidarity, and soon begin to divide as they return to old habits of fending for themselves as individuals only. Basilia, an attractive girl victimized by the boss's lasciviousness, refers to the men of the town as cowards, and adds furthermore: "Father, in this town there are many men all by themselves. If they'd unite, they wouldn't be alone anymore" (p. 160). Unable to stand united, and reminded of the incident in which the *cacique* destroyed the olive crop, the peasantry is afraid to demand fair wages. The feudal power structure prevails, and the bitter reality expressed by Basilia becomes an unanswered challenge to those who almost willingly accept their fate.

II *Techniques*

As in *The Treadmill, The Others,* and *The Current,* Romero employs a circular structure, with fifty-three brief chapters like spokes on a wheel (or buckets on the treadmill) whose axis is the "presence" of the *cacique*. Structurally, the novel is most similar to *The Others,* in that several chapters are devoted to one place or one personage, thus developing in greater depth the major characters of the novel. Another similarity to his previous novels is Romero's technique of temporal condensation in his narrative. The entire action of the novel occurs within approximately thirty-six hours, from the death to the robbery. Such density of time and action creates a sense of simultaneity among the chapters, allowing the author to describe diverse human types and conditions.[6]

The use of dialogue is the dominant means of expression within the novel, and largely replaces the interior monologue and especially the presence of the omniscient narrator of earlier works.[7] Instead of being used excessively, as suggested by some critics,[8] the dialogues serve to reveal with considerable insight the "real" characters who populate Romero's fictional world. The reader is allowed to "discover" the vital essence of each one, perhaps more so than in any of Romero's other "social" novels. As is often the case, the more successful the author is at letting the characters reveal themselves, the more satisfactory the results.

III *Descriptions*

Perhaps Luis Romero's greatest achievement in *The Boss* lies with many of the descriptive passages of the novel. We are referring to those segments which remind the reader of the style of Ramón del Valle-Inclán, an author Romero read during his youth. In his excellent work on the theater of Valle-Inclán, Sumner Greenfield has identified many of the characteristics of Don Ramón's art before World War I;

To the Valle-Inclán of the pre-war period, the plastic values of the human
figure are an unlimited source of aesthetic emotion. From them come, for
example, impressionistic, macabre and satanic effects, evocations of the past
. . ., modernistic exoticisms, and an infinite number of settings and poses.
Implicit in many of these physical stylizations, explicit in others, is a
dehumanizing impulse; shadows, silhouettes, stretched bodies, the focusing
on parts of the body, and, in the period between 1910 and 1913, the puppet,
the mask and the prolonged use of the grotesque.[9]

The traits mentioned by Greenfield when speaking of Valle-Inclán's
art appear in *The Boss*, wherein Luis Romero evinces his preoccupation with the plastic elements of the human figure:

—The whole belly is swollen, and [there are] greenish stains all over the
face. And the rest, except for the belly, [is] very sunken (p. 30).
Isabel lowers her head and covers her face with her hands. Daniel's nostrils
expand and he grimaces with revulsion.
—It stinks here, my love, I'm going into the living room. Just to please you
I accepted this farce. . . . (p. 73)
Don Pablito removes his collar and tie. The tiepin slips [from his hand],
and since it falls on the carpet it doesn't make a sound. He bends to search for
it, feels between his feet and the leg of the table and cannot find it. When he
gets up, his face is congested. (pp. 54–55)

In the first two examples, the appearance of the *cacique's* corpse is
described—color and odor; the third concentrates on certain visual
aspects of Pablito's actions. In all of them, one perceives an attempt to
appeal to the senses of the readers.

The emphasis on the sensorial is further seen in descriptions
tending to dehumanize the characters:

The steps echo on the staircase. Isabel tucks the handkerchief in her
sleeve, Don Pablito dries his hands on his rump, his hands were sweating,
and Don Cristobal, who was ready to open the cigarette case, puts it back in
his side pocket and buttons his coat. (p. 127)

During this scene, a number of simultaneous activities are portrayed.
It seems as if a movie camera were capturing such an undignified
gesture as Pablito's wiping of his hands on his rump. For Valle-Inclán
descriptions are often motivated by a dehumanizing impulse; what is
described in the previous quotation is somewhat static, a characteristic which tends to make us forget the human traits of the personages.[10]

Rodolfo Cardona and Anthony N. Zahareas's comments on the *esperpento*, an art form in which Valle-Inclán succeeds in integrating style "with moral, psychological, historical, aesthetic and social content,"[11] are useful in our comparison of the style of the two writers. According to these critics, there are four basic characteristics of the *esperpento:* "First, and regardless of how artificial it is, the style which deforms into grotesque caricature the human and the Iberic, emanates from an historical circumstance. . . . Second, as an exposé of the lamentable state of human nature, the *esperpento* opposes the [presence of the] tragic [in modern society]. . . . Third, the most characteristic formal elements of the *esperpento* are the dramatic and the theatrical. . . . Scene and characters, stage directions and dialogue, word and gesture, serve to project nothing less than "the miserable life of Spain." . . . Fourth . . ., Valle-Inclán [saw] the absurd consequences of human existence and paint[ed] life as nonsensical. . . .[12]

In *The Boss* the techniques of character distortion and dehumanization convey implicit criticism of the traditional power structure of rural Spanish society. The *cacique,* his children, Don Froilán, Don Eloy, and others represent a regime of exploitation for which Luis Romero shows no sympathy whatsoever. In *The Boss* the novelist does not moralize: he allows his style to express his displeasure. The following two examples should serve to document our interpretation.

In the middle of the novel, Don Froilán expresses his view that oppression should not end with the death of the boss, but should continue at the hands of a new group (that is, Froilán and his henchmen). The paragraphs following Don Froilán's comments artfully describe the reaction of those listening to him:

A murmur of agreement follows the words of Don Froilán. Zabala stretches, crosses his legs, grimaces, shows his teeth to his fangs as he smiles.

Don Eloy breathes hard, places both feet on the floor and with his elbows on his knees bends forward, disguises a belch as he covers his mouth with the back of his hand, and raises his head to watch those around him. (pp. 185–86)

Both Zabala and Don Eloy are described as animals. In the case of Zabala, the animalization—a technique typical of Valle-Inclán—has to do with his teeth. Don Eloy, on the other hand, is seen as a bull preparing to fight: breathing hard, with his body contracted, his head high, and his feet firmly on the ground. This adds a touch of the grotesque. The behavior of Zabala and Don Eloy serves to illustrate the true implication of what Don Froilán has been saying: all of them will behave as beasts as they replace the *cacique*.

The second example describes the governor as he arrives at the funeral: "The governor takes his hat off and wipes the sweat from his brow. He then briefly inserts his little finger in one of the orifices of his nose; he blows his nose and places his handkerchief in his pocket . . ." (p. 259). The disparity between what is expected of a governor and what he does (the cleansing of his nose with his finger) is an implicit condemnation of what this man represents; he has come to pay homage to the deceased, a man who oppressed the very people the governor was supposed to serve.

The examples we have used in our discussion are related to the first three characteristics of the *esperpento* given by professors Cardona and Zahareas. It is through his style that Romero provides a deformed view of an historical institution that he opposes, *caciquismo*, or bossism. The characters lack sufficient dignity to be considered tragic in a classical sense. The tragedy of their lives can be perceived only by an aesthetics of deformation.[13] The most typical trait in the descriptions we have considered is the use of dramatic gestures by the personages, gestures that serve to reveal their negative elements.

In this novel, Luis Romero moves from deformation to absurdity, this being the fourth characteristic attributed by Cardona and Zahareas to the *esperpento*. It is in an absurdist vein that the reader views Aquilino's two monkeys laughing as he hits himself on the head (p. 19) and that we witness the carpenter's discussion of the coffin; ". . . did you measure him? Measure him? Why? We are going to make a big suit for him, the looser the better. Tight clothes do not look good; they're not in style" (p. 29).

The similarities perceived thus far between Valle-Inclán's art and the style of *The Boss* are somewhat rudimentary. Romero's novel was not intended to be an *esperpento*, but had Romero attempted to write an *esperpento*, *The Boss* would be, artistically speaking, a better novel.[14] Nevertheless, it is to Romero's credit that his use of descriptive passages in this work recalls Valle-Inclán. By means of them, he avoids the annoying interference of the narrator, a common trait in many earlier novels.[15] *The Boss* illustrates a new aesthetic dimension in Luis Romero's art.[16] Its importance lies in its ambiguity and the style of certain descriptive passages. By using descriptions to comment, Romero does not have to inform the reader directly, as he did in other works, of the meaning of his novel. In *The Boss* the reader becomes an active participant in the creation of a fictive world.

CHAPTER 8

From Novelistic History to History

THE three works considered in this chapter, *Tres días de julio* (*Three Days in July*), *Desastre en Cartagena* (*Disaster in Cartagena*), and *El final de la guerra* (*The End of the War*), revolve around crucial periods of the Spanish Civil War. In them, we find a shift in emphasis, from "novelized" history to history itself, as the writer Luis Romero turns from fiction to history. *Three Days in July* and *Disaster in Cartagena* have been praised by critics as historical narratives which depend on techniques appropriate to the novel.[1] Luis Romero himself has said that "it is true that literature has limits, but it also has at its disposal very efficient resources which in this case I am using for the writing of history."[2] In short, the two works we are about to consider are, above all, histories of important moments in the Spanish Civil War and *not* examples of the historical novel. They therefore lack that balance which according to Benito Pérez Galdós should exist "between the exactness and beauty of the reproduction" of life.[3]

Historical accuracy was Romero's chief objective in *Three Days in July* and *Disaster in Cartagena*, for he was concerned with writing chronicles and not original literary works of great merit.[4] It should be noted, however, that regardless of its lack of commitment concerning aesthetic matters, Romero's novelistic history has much in common with the historical novel. Like the historical novel, novelistic history "takes a modern reader straight into another time; it shows how men and women (some of them, at any rate) thought and spoke, the problems of their world, the ideals they cherished; it illuminates and sometimes instructs."[5] To Romero, however, his novelistic history is, above all, history: it must have historical truth.[6] Romero's historical inclination culminates in his most recent book, *The End of the War*, where the reader is told that the writer "abandons the literary formula" used in *Three Days in July* and *Disaster in Cartagena*.[7] In doing this, Romero is placing greater emphasis on a continuing

103

preoccupation of these last two works: the avoidance of aesthetic and moral considerations that "may interfere with the photographic quality [the authenticity] of any piece of literature"[8] As we study the basic characteristics of *Three Days in July*, *Disaster in Cartagena*, and *The End of the War*, Romero's historical purpose should be kept in mind, as it is essential to the evaluation of these works.

I Three Days in July

Published in 1967, *Three Days in July* is the result of three years of intensive research by the author. The title refers to the first three days of the Spanish Civil War (July 18–20, 1936), a period which begins with great confusion and apprehension caused by news of mutiny by the Spanish army in Morocco. Selecting cities which are important from the viewpoint of the history of the war, and drawing upon the full gamut of personalities involved in the political decisions and military confrontations, Romero provides a vast literary panorama of the events of those seventy-two hours. Although most of his characters were actual participants in the conflict, Romero has added a number of fictional personages and situations in an attempt to convey the complexity and the pervasiveness of the struggle in the lives of the Spanish people. In order that the reader may comprehend so many events, the author utilizes a series of short, rapid scenes which emphasize the direct or indirect presentation of a character or event. Since the novel is divided into three chapters, one for each day, the action in different cities develops in a simultaneous, if somewhat chaotic, fashion. This chaos reflects the general disorientation which characterized Spain during the first moments of the Civil War.[9]

On the first day, sporadic news announcements, official reports, and rumors abound concerning the military revolt. Government politicians, labor leaders, and pro-government army officers anxiously await word that the revolt has been crushed, while rebellious factions are ready to act in support of the barracks uprising. The major question is, has General Franco succeeded in his African campaign, and is there sufficient military support of the Republican government to withstand the' attack by dissident forces? Labor and leftist party leaders urge President Azaña to arm the "people" against the Fascists, but the government fears the potential power of the more radical groups should they obtain access to the military arsenal. The second day is characterized by a show of unity and strength from the rebels, in contrast to the disorganization and confusion on the part of the progovernment forces. Both sides develop strategies to gain an advantage in what appears to be inevitable bloodshed. Radio and press reports are contradictory, and there is a sense of uneasy anticipation in government circles, the barracks, the street. Of crucial importance is the question of army loyalty in Madrid and Barcelona. But consistently, rebellious officers begin to gain the upper hand in their own internal struggle for power. By the third day the fighting has broken out, and more and more civilians are drawn into the conflict. Soldiers in the Madrid "Montaña Barracks" soon find themselves trapped in their headquarters and suffer tremendous losses to the enemy. Barcelona remains under government control after much fighting with the army. Throughout the country the battle continues to gather momentum. Is this the beginning of a costly and disastrous Civil War? This question, raised repeatedly by President Azaña and other characters, has been answered by history, and becomes an ironic statement about the ignorance of man as he faces the agony and suffering of war.[10]

Although the work presents a panoramic view of the struggle, it does so by means of the accumulation of individual histories, vignettes designed to reveal the fears and hopes of the Spanish people. Sketches of figures such as General Franco, President Azaña, Minister of War Casares Quiroga, labor leader Francisco Largo Caballero, rebel general Queipo de Llano and loyalist Núñez del Prado, conservative leader of the Falange José Antonio Primo de Rivera, colonels, workers, businessmen, anarchists, and peasants represent only a fraction of the exhaustive list of participants in the events of these three historical days. Romero treats many of the most important characters and the moments they lived during such difficult times in a few brief scenes, thus creating a dramatic build-up of tension and uncertainty while maintaining the appearance of chronological simultaneity among events.

The reader is able to experience the suspense of Republican official Arturo Menéndez's ill-fated trip to Madrid, during which he is captured before being able to deliver a crucial intelligence report to government leaders. One appreciates the difficulty of General Queipo de Llano's personal decision to abandon the Republican cause. Interesting characters include, for example, legionnaire Gassols who orders a squadron of airplanes to land at Sevilla even though the airport may be controlled by Republican forces, and "Manías," a young Communist lad who hawks papers for the *Worker's World* and is caught up in the excitement of the siege of the "Montaña Barracks" in Madrid, only to be cut down by the retaliatory machine-gun fire from the army headquarters.[11] Especially noteworthy are the painstaking, step-by-step descriptions of the siege of the "Montaña Barracks" and the struggle for the control of Barcelona.[12]

The most controversial and important questions concerning *Three Days in July* involve its structure and, more basically, its genre. Seen strictly as a novel,[13] the work is seriously hampered by the author's insistence on detail in every aspect of the world he presents: rooms, buildings, clothes, personal habits, friends, family, and most of all, names. The work is filled with names both fictional and historical, a technique which, at its worst, takes on the appearance of the index of a history book.[14] Particularly in the presentation of the first day, the combination of excessive details and the tedious repetition of similar events and characters challenges only the most avid enthusiast for information about the Civil War. If the book is judged as a novel, its overabundance of detail is a serious defect.[15]

Romero explains in his prologue to *Three Days in July* that the work was conceived and realized as a "chronicle," a "novelized" history, which is carefully written with the purpose of analyzing and documenting as objectively as possible the various human and political factors of the initial days of the war. The author further insists that in this work he has sacrificed style for historical accuracy and completeness of documentation. Entire dialogues are copied from statements made by the actual participants in events re-created in the work; others were submitted by the author to witnesses or participants for verifications of accuracy and objectivity. Segments of radio broadcasts, letters, newspaper articles, and other documents are reproduced exactly.[16]

The effort to emphasize history notwithstanding, *Three Days in July* does not lack important structural and stylistic features common to the novel, an art form which Romero the novelist instinctively knew was capable of providing a more authentic and profound view of the Civil War.[17] When not bogged down by facts and details, or by the chaotic and seemingly disorganized order of events, the rapid movement from place to place and from character to character effectively re-creates the kind of bewildered confusion that plagued the Spanish people during those three days. Two means of expression predominate within the narrative fragments: dialogue and indirect interior monologue, techniques which have been constants in Romero's fictional works since *The Treadmill.* Of the two, the indirect interior monologue warrants special attention, for it could be argued that this technique is not only used to present the thoughts of the characters, but also allows the omniscient narrator to interpret what is happening. As the omniscient narrator gives us the thoughts of Manuel Azaña, he proceeds to comment on the character's disorientation: "Manuel Azaña, President of the Spanish Republic, does not know how to answer these questions that move, disquiet and frighten him" (p. 617). At another point, the narrator's commentary is more direct as he describes the attitudes of the inhabitants of Burgos during a rally in the town square (p. 309). In both instances the reader is uncertain as to the identity of the speaker: we cannot be totally sure as to whether we are witnessing the thoughts of a character, transmitted to us by an omniscient narrator as part of the indirect interior monologue, or if we are simply listening to the opinions of this same narrator (and not the character).[18]

José Luis Cano (p. 9) has stressed the use of the present tense throughout the work as a successful attempt to represent simultaneity of action and to impart a sense of immediacy to events and decisions. But often the dialogue is contrived to include pertinent historical information which only reduces spontaneity and literary verisimilitude. This problem is alleviated somewhat in the final chapter because speculation about and anticipation of armed revolt (no movement, repetition of similar conversations) is followed by the violent action and development (movement in place and time) of the uprising. Another aspect of *Three Days in July*, resulting from its historical nature and its having novelistic overtones, is the work's open-endedness. There are no clues as to the direction the conflict will take. Throughout the book a vital concern is the question of the validity of information, because conflicting reports leave everyone uncertain and anxious about the future. What *is* certain in *Three Days in July* is that there are feelings of hatred and bitterness, which themselves lead to unprecedented levels of violence and retribution, and point to the virtual inevitability of civil war.[19]

The work ends almost as it began, in the presidential palace, as President Azaña pauses to consider the events of the preceding three days. His questions are excruciatingly ironic for the reader familiar with the history of the war and the postwar years in Spain. Viewing the smoke from the fires that burn in the capital city, the president asks if this is the beginning of the horror of a civil war. No one is as yet sure, confusion still reigns, and the historian-novelist remains objective by not weighting the balance on one side or the other. The work closes as the country braces itself for the most devastating event in its entire history, one in which all participants were victims of the inhumanity of war.

II   Disaster in Cartagena

If there is any question as to whether *Three Days in July* is an historical novel or a novelistic history, there is no doubt about the second of Romero's three books on the Civil War, *Disaster in Cartagena* (1971).[20] The author's goal, as stated in the preface to the book, is to achieve the "objective truth" (p. 10) concerning the political and military conflict in Cartagena from March 4 to March 7, 1939, not long before the end of the three-year war. Such is Romero's concern for historical accuracy that he adopts the use of dialogue to bring out certain subtleties of atmosphere and interpersonal conflict that the traditional history text would be incapable of expressing as effectively. But at the same time, the historian-novelist explains that his dialogues have not been conceived or written so much as "literary" selections as historical documents, because he reproduces directly from his notes and conversations the words of actual participants or witnesses to the events he describes.[21] *Disaster in Cartagena* is clearly a history book in which the author attempts to disentangle confusion and misconceptions as to this important period.

Disaster in Cartagena seeks to depict the last days of the war, to convey the chaotic atmosphere which prevailed once the end of the war was perceived as imminent. When President Negrín selects avowed Communist Francisco Galán to direct the Republican forces against a possible insurrection in Cartagena, the appointment only precipitates the loss of support within Republican ranks. When Galán is taken prisoner, confusion and uncertainty reign, for now there is a "civil war" within a Civil War, and no one among the Republicans is sure of the loyalties of his comrades. Many military men, from officers to foot soldiers, are resigned to defeat; their only desire is to avoid more suffering and bloodshed. But there are still those who are willing to fight desperately for the Republican cause, especially the committed Communists whose influence on the Republican side is challenged by the insurrectionists. Out of this conflict come stories of human beings, their moments of hope and despair, of glory and infamy. Everyone is a victim of the cruel and impersonal effects of war, which are made even more unfortunate because it is a disastrous struggle of a people against itself.

In several ways the development of the "historical" text (as opposed to *Three Days in July*, which combines more successful literary techniques with the historical narrative) is apparent in *Disaster in Cartagena*. In the former work a number of personal histories were traced throughout the length of the book, but in *Disaster in Cartagena* only a few characters stand out as persons. The most important of these is Coronel Gerardo Armentia Palacios, a Republican officer who, according to other historians, committed suicide. Romero refutes that idea. In *Disaster in Cartagena*, the valiant officer is mortally wounded in a gun battle at his headquarters. The emphasis on Armentia is primarily due to Romero's desire for historical accuracy. Other participants in the struggle, such as Francisco Galán and Republican general Rafael Barrionuevo, who became titular head of the insurrectionists, are treated in some detail, but are not memorable figures. The emphasis is clearly on events rather than characters, as one might expect in an historical work regarding a particular military conflict, a case study of the war. In *Three Days in July* the author concentrates on the personal lives of characters from all levels of Spanish society in order to depict the mood of separation and alienation which led to the war. The aim of *Disaster in Cartagena* is to clarify facts, to explain what happened in a particular struggle. Individual histories are subordinate to the clarification of events during the three days.

There is an omniscient narrator in *Disaster in Cartagena*. His role is more important than in *Three Days in July*, especially during the second half of the work. Although Romero continues to employ indirect interior monologue as a basic narrative technique in *Disaster in Cartagena*, the omniscience of the narrator is used extensively to provide information about the characters and to reveal facts of which they themselves are unaware. For example, the narrator explains that General Barrionuevo and other rebels are not aware of their own strength. The narrator also describes the insurrectionists as weak and of dubious loyalty: "General Barrionuevo and those who support him, with greater or lesser efficiency, enthusiasm, and sincerity, are unaware of the forces at their own disposal, weak forces, scattered, and subject to changes in mood according to convenience and opportunity" (p. 200). In another instance, the narrator interprets the feelings of all the insurrectionists and their disillusionment over the slow advance of the Nationalist forces: "Depression has begun to set in among the rebels of the arsenal and even more so among those who accepted things without commitment because they thought that the war was ending and that there was no enemy. Rather than rebel against the duly constituted power they believed themselves destined to maintain order in the final, difficult, and painstaking step towards definitive peace. . . . Events are different than they believed" (p. 226).

Romero makes astute use of historical documents, and particularly of telegrams sent between Cartagena and the Nationalist headquarters at Burgos, which was under the personal direction of Franco. The device is effective, for nothing could be more historically accurate than the exact reproduction of these messages; on the other hand, while the narrative thus gains in terseness in the second half of the work, it must necessarily sacrifice some of the effectiveness of description found in the earlier parts.[22] The description becomes very direct; sentences are often shortened and sometimes either the verb or subject is eliminated: "They're advancing from various directions. The decision was taken beforehand: it must be carried out without delay. Escape to submarine C–2" (p. 226). The book thus assumes the character of a document, a collection of facts which are to be used in the objective analysis of historical events.[23] In *Disaster in Cartagena* Romero provides the results of years of painstaking work devoted to the effort to understand the nature of the Cartagena insurrection. It is on the accuracy and perceptiveness of its observations that the book should be judged, but it must be remembered that the framework for the historical analysis is still a literary one, and that *Disaster in Cartagena* uses novelistic structure and techniques to convey history in a way that the history text does not.

III   The End of the War

With *The End of the War* (1976), Luis Romero abandons the presentation of history by means of techniques normally associated with the novel. *The End of the War* is a history book that attempts to describe and comment upon the last four days of the Civil War (March 29–April 1, 1939), and the events leading to its conclusion (p. 11).[24] In this work Romero's chief motive is to be historically accurate (p. 31) and to strive for an "objective"—as opposed to literary—truth. Of necessity, however, Romero is unable to describe historical events with complete detachment. On numerous occasions he employs the first-person singular or plural to present his perception of history. The intervention of the first-person narrator permits him to explain the difficulties he faced in the analysis of conflicting accounts of a single event (for example, see pp. 53–54).

Even though the overall conception of *The End of the War* is obviously different from *Three Days in July* and *Disaster in Cartagena,* Romero believes these three works to be essentially similar (pp. 16 and 56). This attitude is logical if one stops to consider that for Luis Romero his last three books are *histories,* a fact not altered by his use of different means of expression. One might conclude that to Romero *Disaster in Cartagena,* a work which has a literary framework, is as historical concerning the events that took place in that town between March 4 and March 7, 1939, as is the discussion of these same incidents that appears in *The End of the War* (pp. 194–219, 229–47, and 311–19). Perhaps his view that accounts that appear dissimilar to the reader are in fact comparable can be understood more fully if we realize that for Luis Romero an historical event may acquire novelistic dimensions: "Regardless of the dynamism of the events in Cartagena and of their *almost* novelistic elements . . ." (p. 221, our italics). The word "almost" in this quotation reaffirms our belief that very often Luis Romero is unsure as to what differentiates history from fiction: the artist in this case appears not to be at the helm of his craft.

Throughout this chapter we have considered Romero's change of emphasis in *Three Days in July, Disaster in Cartagena,* and *The End of the War.* From "novelized" history he has moved to history itself. In doing this, Romero's development as a novelist has come to a halt; his preoccupations with history have led him to artistic stagnation (and we refer not only to *The End of the War*).[25] As we have mentioned before in this chapter, the concern with history has become an obstacle to the development of Luis Romero, the novelist. His obsession with the presentation of facts has inhibited those creative abilities documented in *The Treadmill* and *The Boss.*[26]

CHAPTER 9

Summary and Conclusions

LUIS Romero's place in the history of Spanish literature must be determined primarily by the worth of his novels and short stories. Although he has cultivated other genres, his best efforts lie within the field of fiction. Among the Spanish post–Civil War novelists, he does not rank as highly as Cela, Delibes, Goytisolo, and Martín-Santos, for example. His place to date is that of a good writer whose work is comparable in quality to that of other important members of his generation (for instance, Gironella, Aldecoa, Sender, Laforet, and Matute). In our study of Romero's works we have seen that certain traits predominate. Thematically he is concerned with man's existential problems: solitude, the emptiness of life, the lack of communication with other human beings, society's oppressiveness toward the individual, social injustice, man's desire to escape from a hostile environment. To enhance the impact of these themes on the reader, they are presented from individual and collective perspectives.

From a technical point of view Romero has demonstrated a preoccupation with the integration of themes and techniques. His cannot be labeled an extraordinary artistic contribution to the state of the art; however, Romero was not, as a rule, concerned with technical innovation. Within his production we discern a certain development. In comparison with *The Treadmill*, one of his best novels, *Letter from the Past* represents a step backward. *The Old Voices*, his third novel, becomes a synthesis of sorts in the use of the individual and generic perspectives (combining narrative viewpoints used in the first two novels). With *The Others* and *The Current*, as was the case with *The Treadmill*, Romero continues his use of variations of the "capsular novel," a type of fragmentary fiction that through its structure projects the human isolation and alienation of its characters. *Shadows from Beyond* and *Tudá* are very dissimilar collections of short stories. The former is experimental in nature and at times successful in its attempt to expand Romero's horizons as a writer; the latter is extremely traditional insofar as narrative techniques are concerned. For the most part *Tudá* is a monotonous work, a trait shared with Romero's next novel, *Christmas Eve*. The overt symbolism that prevails in *Christmas Eve* is to a large measure responsible for its artistic failure. Romero's latest novel, *The Boss*, is along with *The Treadmill* his best work to date. The outstanding feature of this novel is its description of the human figure, descriptions reminiscent of Valle-Inclán's grotesque distortions. Romero's most recent works, *Three Days in July, Disaster in Cartagena,* and *The End of the War*, are studies of different moments of the Spanish Civil War. In the first two, he attempts to incorporate novelistic techniques in his presentation of history. From a literary perspective, unfortunately, his inability to distinguish clearly between history and fiction in the works leads Romero to abandon progressively his commitment to the novel and to become more of an historian than a novelist. The desire to write historical works has thus led to an interruption in his career as a creative writer.

Among the techniques most often used by Romero in his writings are different varieties of interior monologues, means of expression which he considers most effective in the presentation of man's personal dilemmas.[1] Also significant is Romero's ability to choose for many of his works the structure most suitable for the expression of their thematic objectives (the outstanding example is *The Treadmill*). Success, however, is often accompanied by failure. Perhaps Romero's most evident artistic shortcoming lies in the intervention of the narrator in the events of a work. This unnecessary intrusion serves to clarify the objectives of the author at the expense of that ambiguity present in most great literary works. It is to be hoped that as Luis Romero continues his career as a writer, he will return to fiction and avoid those literary shortcomings we have identified in our book.

Notes and References

Chapter One

1. Ignacio Soldevila-Durante, "Entrevista a Luis Romero," unpublished document, transcribed by José Varela Muñóz, March 13, 1965, p. 1.
2. Luis Romero, "El autor y su obra," *La noria* (Barcelona: Cuento de lectores, 1971), n.p.
3. Soldevila-Durante, p. 3 and Rafael Borras Betriu, "Galería de retratos. Luis Romero," *La Jirafa*, No. 10 (1958), p. 9.
4. "El autor y su obra."
5. Luis González-del-Valle and Antolín González-del-Valle, "Entrevista a Luis Romero," unpublished document, October 1973, p. 6.
6. Ibid.
7. "El autor y su obra."
8. Soldevila-Durante, pp. 5-6.
9. "El autor y su obra."
10. Salvador Paniker, "Luis Romero," *Conversaciones en Cataluña* (Barcelona: Editorial Kairos, 1966), p. 213.
11. Generally speaking, Romero has chosen not to discuss his life publicly out of a deep sense of privacy. On this subject see his comments on "Perfiles humanos de la actividad aseguradora," lecture delivered in June 1963 to celebrate the end of the academic year 1962–1963 at the Escuela Profesional del Sindicato del Seguro, pp. 15–16.
12. Soldevila-Durante, p. 50. Joaquín de Entrambasaguas's belief that Romero's life is important in his writings gains credence as we examine his activities as a soldier and proceed to contrast them with such works as *Tudá, Tres días de julio, Desastre en Cartagena,* and *El final de la guerra* (all to be studied in our book). See "Luis Romero," *Las mejores novelas contemporáneas,* Vol. 12 (Barcelona: Editorial Planeta, 1971), p. 995.
13. "Perfiles humanos de la actividad aseguradora," p. 1.
14. Ibid., p. 20.
15. "El autor y su obra." It should be noted that Romero has traveled extensively outside Spain (to Germany and Russia during World War II, and to France, Italy, England, Czechoslovakia, Argentina, and Mexico). On this subject see "El autor y su obra;" Soldevila-Durante, p. 21; and Juan Illa Morell, "Luis Romero," *Revista Vallés* (February 21, 1970).
16. "Perfiles humanos de la actividad aseguradora," p. 18.
17. "El autor y su obra."
18. Ibid.

19. Ibid. A different date is given by Illa Morell.

20. On December 10, 1955, Romero and his wife had a son, Javier. Since their return to Spain, they have lived very private lives.

21. Soldevila-Durante, p. 17; "El autor y su obra;" Illa Morell; and *Quien es quien en las letras españolas* (Madrid: Instituto Nacional del Libro Español, 1969), pp. 358–59.

22. The stories are "J. J. Goldemberg" and "Camallarg i la ciencia nuclear."

23. Borras Betriu, p. 9.

24. This estimate was made by Romero in a letter to us dated February 7, 1975.

25. We have not been able to locate these translations. Romero informed us of them in a letter dated March 1, 1971.

26. Throughout his life Romero has been an admirer of painters. This interest has taken him to many prominent European museums (in Madrid, Barcelona, Paris, and London) and in part explains his friendship with such distinguished painters of our century as Dalí, Tharrats, Cuixart, Guinovart, Tapies. Romero discusses this with Soldevila-Durante, pp. 6–7.

27. Romero has discussed his essays with us in letters dated February 7, 1975, and March 1, 1975.

28. Romero refers to all of this in a letter dated March 1, 1975. See also Entrambasaguas, p. 997, and Soldevila-Durante, pp. 15–16, 22.

29. This information was given to us by Beth A. Scott, Membership Librarian of The Hispanic Society of America, in a letter dated July 30, 1975.

30. Soldevila-Durante, p. 43. Also, Paniker, p. 215; "Perfiles humanos en la actividad aseguradora," p. 17; and Bartolomé Mostaza, "Luis Romero: Su obra y su actitud," *El libro español*, 7 (February 1964), p. 46.

31. Luis Romero, "Aviso que podría parecer innecesario," *Las viejas voces* (Barcelona: Editorial Exito, S.A., 1955), p. 5.

32. Luis Romero, "El libro, el autor y el editor," lecture delivered at the Biblioteca Central de Barcelona, April 24, 1967, p. 57. Romero adds that perhaps the artist and the man of letters are ahead of the sociologist, economist, and politician in mankind's march toward social progress (p. 58).

33. Francisco Olmos García, "La novela y los novelistas españoles de hoy," *Cuadernos Americanos*, 129 (July-August 1963), pp. 215–16. See as well Luis González-del-Valle and Antolín González-del-Valle, "Entrevista a Luis Romero," *Hispania*, 58 (March 1975), p. 215; "El escritor y su espejo. Luis Romero," *ABC* (September 16, 1965); and Soldevila-Durante, p. 41.

34. Luis Romero, "Prólogo," *Los otros* (Barcelona: Ediciones Destino, 1956), p. 9.

35. Soldevila-Durante, pp. 35, 40–41.

36. Ibid., p. 43.

37. *Los otros*, p. 9, and *Las viejas voces*, p. 6. The notion that characters should be independent of their creator is one that appears to disturb Luis Romero, as seen in his comments to Soldevila-Durante, p. 43. There he

seems to say that the concern for character independence is more than
anything else a preoccupation of our time, perhaps a literary fad, and not a
requirement for authentic and important fiction.
    38. Manuel Arce, "En una taberna con Luis Romero," *Índice de Artes y
Letras*, 52 (June 15, 1952), p. 6.
    39. "Perfiles humanos en la actividad aseguradora," p. 17, and González-
del-Valle, *Hispania*, pp. 215–16.
    40. Mostaza, p. 46.
    41. José Luis Cano, "Charlas en *Insula*. Luis Romero," *Insula*, 110
(February 15, 1955), p. 8, and Soldevila-Durante, pp. 42–43.

Chapter Three

    1. In an interview with Juan Illa Morell entitled "Luis Romero," *Revista
Vallés* (February 21, 1970), Romero recalls that after receiving the Nadal
Prize, "I have lived exclusively from literature, that is, from the income that
my books have produced, and I think that in those days [in the 1950s], if not
the only one, I was one of only a very few Spanish writers who, with nothing
more than a typewriter, maintained a family and enjoyed the freedom and
independence that a writer needs. . . ."
    2. In addition to the critical bibliography on Romero, more than twenty
interviews add insight into his view of life and literature. See the Selected
Bibliography.
    3. Romero remarks that when *The Treadmill* was published in French
translation, many Parisians asked him about the buildings and avenues of
Barcelona as presented in the novel. See "Un éxito de Luis Romero,"
Destino, 1246 (June 24, 1961). Juan Luis Alborg *Índice de artes y letras*, 97
[February 1957], p. 30) mentions the interest in Barcelona concerning the
so-called "novel of Barcelona."
    4. Critical references to *The Treadmill* include the following: Andrés
Amorós, *Introducción a la novela contemporánea* (Madrid: Anaya, 1971), p.
128; Pablo Gil Casado, *La novela social española (1942–1968)* (Barcelona:
Editorial Seix Barral, S.A., 1968), pp. 263–64; Eugenio G. de Nora, *La
novela española contemporánea*, Vol. 3, 2nd ed. (Madrid: Editorial Gredos,
1970), pp. 151–51; Juan Luis Alborg, *Hora actual de la novela española*, Vol.
2 (Madrid: Taurus, 1962), p. 313; Antonio Iglesias Laguna, *Treinta años de
novela española (1938—1968)*, Vol. 1 (Madrid: Editorial "Prensa Española,"
(1969), p. 298; Fernando Guillermo de Castro, "Libros. *La noria*," *Indice de
artes y letras*, 7, no. 52 (June 1952); José María Castellet, *Notas sobre
literatura española contemporánea* (Barcelona: Ediciones Laye, 1955), pp.
55–57; José Luis Cano, book review of *La noria*, *Insula*, 78 (June 15, 1952);
Antonio Vilanova, "*La noria*, de Luis Romero," *Destino*, 827 (June 1953);
William John Grupp, "Two Novels by Luis Romero," *Hispania*, 39 (1956),
pp. 201–203; Olga P. Ferrer, "La literatura tremendista y su nexo con el
existencialismo," *Revista Hispánica Moderna*, 22 (1956), p. 303; José Cor-

rales Egea, *La novela española actual* (Madrid: Editorial Cuadernos para el Diálogo, S.A., 1971), p. 161; J. Luis Castillo-Puche, *"La noria y sus treinta y siete cangilones,"* *Correo literatio* (September 15, 1952), p. 4; Joaquín de Entrambasaguas, *Las mejores novelas contemporáneas,* Vol. 12 (Barcelona: Editorial Planeta, 1971), pp. 999—1004; and Francisco Yndurain, *"Novelas y novelistas españoles 1936–1952,"* *Revista di Letterature Moderne e Comparate,* 3(1952), p. 279.

    5. See especially Iglesias Laguna, p. 298, Entrambasaguas, p. 1001, and Grupp, p. 201.

    6. We have chosen to translate the title as *The Treadmill* for the benefit of English-language speakers who may have difficulty in visualizing the chain-pump apparatus. The term also refers to the *"Ferris Wheel."*

    7. Castellet (p. 56) has reacted negatively to the repetitious manner of presenting the characters, stating that they differ only in the particular circumstances in which they live. Rather than a defect, we consider this a successful technique.

    8. Alborg (p. 313), Castillo-Puche (p. 4), and Castro criticize the fact that in *The Treadmill* only one chapter is devoted to each character. In their view the personages are not properly developed, the result of which, according to Alborg, is the reader's feeling of being "defrauded." The limitations of Romero's method lead Alborg to make an even stronger statement: "The fact is that *The Treadmill,* despite the possibilities of the simile of the chain pump, is not really a "treadmill": the pump turns and returns "a thousand and one" times in its fateful orbit, and its buckets rust and get moldy in the endless task of drawing water from the well. But in Romero's *The Treadmill* the element of "return" is missing; his characters would be more properly compared to passing clouds, impossible to retain in the winglike outline of their form, or to flocks of birds, glimpsed in all their beauty and fragility, but only fleetingly retained in our mind's eye." What Alborg does not take into account is that the "simile" of the chain pump cannot function with a more detailed development of characters because in the novel they are seen only briefly. The repetitive effect is achieved in the novel when they become associated with humanity. That is to say, what they are today, others will be, and others, and others. . . . Interestingly enough, Alborg later refers indirectly to the generic quality of the work: ". . . the novel reflects real-life situations in any of our large urban centers" (p. 314).

    9. Quotations and references to *The Treadmill* are from the 7th ed. (Barcelona: Ediciones Destino, 1968).

    10. Grupp (p. 202) recognizes that the characters of *The Treadmill* represent not only the people of Barcelona, or of Spain, but all people.

    11. Another theme in the novel is social injustice. Mercedes's son, for example, feels that stealing is the only way in which he can maintain even a minimal standard of living (p. 138). Implicitly, of course, the basic problems as presented in *The Treadmill* have their roots in society. However, Romero is more concerned with the effects that society exercises on the individual

than with the difficult social condition, although, as Andrés Amorós says (p. 128), his vision of society "carries with it implicitly a desire to witness or reform society." See Romero's own comments on this matter in Francisco Olmos García, "La novela y los nevelistas españoles de hoy," *Cuadernos Americanos*, 129 (July-August 1963), p. 215.

12. For further discussion of this topic, see Iglesias Laguna, p. 297, and Olga Ferrer, p. 303.

13. Further elaboration of the importance of sunshine as a gift of God is implied by the title of this last chapter: "Dawn." It is interesting to note that throughout the novel other chapters have titles which directly relate to their content. Some of them, such as "The Verdict," refer to the fundamental motivation of the chapter. In this case the lawyer Carlos Pi awaits the decision of his doctor as to whether or not he has contracted syphilis. For Carlos this verdict is a sentence, since he already feels guilty about his licentious living. Other chapters carry the name of a person, because their primary function is to present a brief study of an individual character (for example, "Raquel").

14. Olmos García, p. 215.

15. "Luis Romero: Su obra y su actitud," *El Libro Español*, 7 (February 1964), p. 46. Something similar has been stated by Romero in his answer to a questionnaire submitted to him by Luis González-del-Valle and Antolín González-del-Valle ("Entrevista a Luis Romero," *Hispania*, 58 [May 1975], pp. 215–16).

16. See the comments by Corrales Egea, p. 161; Nora, pp. 150–51, note 28- and Castellet, p. 55.

17. Gil Casado, p. 263.

18. "Prólogo," *Los Otros* (Barcelona: Ediciones Destino, 1956), p. 9.

19. As can be expected, during this day the people must remember their past and think of their future. Both activities expand the chronological horizons of the work.

20. Two other good examples appear on pp. 271 and 279.

21. Another example appears on p. 10.

22. Something similar takes place on pp. 122 and 124.

23. See the comments made by Gil Casado, pp. 263—64; Iglesias Laguna, p. 298; Castro; and Vilanova. Above all, these writers believe those paragraphs that are enclosed in parentheses and that show a degree of incoherence to be a flaw in the novel.

24. We are using this terminology as it was defined by Robert Humphrey, *Stream of Consciousness in the Modern Novel* (Berkeley and Los Angeles: University of California Press, 1968).

25. Humphrey defines indirect interior monologue in the following fashion: "Indirect interior monologue is, then, that type of interior monologue in which an omniscient author presents unspoken material as if it were directly from the consciousness of a character and, with commentary and description, guides the reader through it" (p. 29).

26. Other places where the narrator appears are pp. 111, 134, 180, and

190. Note also that we do not agree with Grupp, p. 202, according to whom all that is described in the novel emanates from the characters and not the author.

27. Criticism is also directed against hospitals which give preferential treatment to the rich, the Church, and the "social morality" which oppresses the individual.

28. For example, neither Llorach, whose mother dominates him completely, nor Arístides, is to blame for his homosexuality.

29. Romero demonstrates respect for his characters by carefully avoiding "scandalous" language to describe their failings. The lasciviousness of Don Raimundo is discussed with extreme discretion (p. 161).

30. "Aviso que podría parecer innecesario," *Las viejas voces* (Barcelona: Editorial Exito, S.A., 1955), p. 6.

31. "Prólogo," *Los Otros*, p. 9.

32. On direct interior monologue, we refer the reader to Humphrey's discussion:

Direct interior monologue is that type of interior monologue which is represented with negligible author interference and with no auditor assumed. It is the type of monologue that Dujardin is concerned with in his definition. An examination of its special methods reveals: that it presents consciousness directly to the reader with negligible author interference; that is, there is either a complete or near complete disappearance of the author from the page, with his guiding "he said"s and "he thought"s and with his explanatory comments. It should be emphasized that there is no auditor assumed; that is, the character is not speaking to anyone within the fictional scene; nor is the character speaking, in effect, to the reader (as the speaker of a stage monologue is, for example). In short the monologue is represented as being completely candid, as if there were no reader. (p. 25)

The basic difference between the two techniques is that indirect monologue gives to the reader a sense of the author's continuous presence; whereas direct monologue either completely or largely excludes it. This difference in turn admits of special differences, such as the use of third-person instead of first-person point of view; the wider use of descriptive and expository methods to present the monologue; and the possibility of greater coherence and greater surface unity through selection of materials. (p. 29)

33. On the stream of consciousness, Humphrey states:

The greatest problem of the stream-of-consciousness writer is to capture the irrational and incoherent quality of private unuttered consciousness and in doing so still to communicate to his readers. Readers in the twentieth century, after all, expect of language and syntax some kind of empirical order and completeness. Yet, if consciousness is to be represented at all convincingly, the representation must lack to a great degree these very qualities that a reader has a right to expect. . . .
Consequently, the writer of stream-of-consciousness literature has to manage to represent consciousness realistically by maintaining its characteristics of privacy (the

incoherence, discontinuity, and private implications), and he has to manage to communicate something to the reader through this consciousness. (p. 62)

34. On this subject Humphrey says:

The chief technique in controlling the movement of stream of consciousness in fiction has been an application of the principles of psychological free association. . . .
The psyche, which is almost continuously active, cannot be concentrated for very long in its processes, even when it is most strongly willed; when little effort is exerted to concentrate it, its focus remains on any one thing but momentarily. Yet the activity of consciousness must have content, and this is provided for by the power of one thing to suggest another through an association of qualities in common or contrast, wholly, or partially—even to the barest suggestion. Three factors control the association: first, the memory, which is its basis; second, the senses, which guide it; and third, the imagination, which determines its elasticity. (p. 43)

35. A detailed explanation of this term is given by Humphrey on p. 66:

What seems incoherent in the privacy of consciousness is actually only egocentric. The basis for this is the private relationships of the associations. Thus we have again to consider the functioning of free association in stream-of-consciousness fiction. We have seen in a previous chapter that free association is the chief principle by which the movement of any "stream" of consciousness is controlled. It is a stabilizing factor, although a tenuous one. Often in *Ulysses*, for example, the associations are not explained at the time the process is indicated. The explanations may lie hidden several hundred pages separated from the association. Consequently, at the moment the association is made, unless the reader has a remarkable memory, the effect is one of incoherence. There will seem to be simply no logical reason for such a connection. The reason lies in the seeming lack of logic of psychological free association and in the egocentricity with which it functions in the psychic processes.

36. José Luis Cano, p. 6, has dealt with this aspect of the work.

Chapter Four

1. The murder of Claudia might be seen as a suicide in the sense that Claudia controlled the will of her lover and because she too could not bear to continue their sad relationship.

2. At one point the narrator admits his own indifference to the problem of age and mentions Claudia's concern (p. 91). But any gradual development of their contrasting perspectives is lost in the labyrinthine framework of the young man's recollections.

3. William John Grupp, "Two novels by Luis Romero," *Hispania*, 39 (1956), p. 203, and M. Tudela, "*Carta de ayer*, segunda novela de Luis Romero," *Cuadernos Hispanoamericanos*, 17, No. 44 (1953), p. 262.

4. Other examples of foreshadowing appear on pp. 10, 12, 19, 21, 23, 65, 112, 147, 198, 209, 220, 244.

5. Quotations and references to *The Old Voices* are from the edition published in Barcelona by the Editorial Exito, S.A., in 1955.

6. Other examples appear on pp. 29, 121, 134, 174.

7. See as well p. 115.

8. See pp. 11, 13, 170–71, 196–97.

Chapter Five

1. All quotations and references are to the first edition of *Los Otros* (Barcelona: Ediciones Destino, 1956).

2. Irony is employed to advantage in the novel in other ways as well. Many times it is used to relieve the nervous tension of the chase. In one passage, for example, the thief complains that his victim is late for their "appointment," when obviously there was no such arrangement (see p. 84).

3. Manuel de Cerezales, in his review of *The Others* (*Informaciones* [Madrid], May 19, 1956), offers perhaps the best summary of the social dimension of the novel: ". . . On one side are the privileged, the rich and powerful who own everything and who are indifferent to the suffering and poverty of the weak, and on the other side are the unjustly overlooked workers with miserable salaries, humble employees, small businessmen without the means to survive in the business world." The factory owner is representative of the first class, and the thief of the latter.

4. According to Gil Casado, p. 269, the prolonged agony of the thief is tedious, and he does not consider this effect appropriate.

5. In his "Prologue" to *The Others*, Romero makes reference to having intervened in the action of the novel. As is obvious from the following quote, the author does not realize that his participation in the novel detracts from its artistic qualities: ". . . I have allowed my characters to express themselves with freedom, and only once in a while—such are the defects or privileges of the trade—the opinion of the novelist appears blended with those of the character or he slips in a comment almost by accident" (p. 9).

6. *La Corriente* (Barcelona: Ediciones Destino, 1962).

7. Little criticism has been written about *The Current*. Antonio Vilanova suggests that *The Current* might be rightly considered "volume two" of its companion novel *The Treadmill* ("*La Corriente* de Luis Romero," *Destino*, No. 1304 [August 4, 1962], p. 36). José R. Marra-López maintains that *The Current* is simply a sequel or continuation of *The Treadmill (Insula*, No. 192 [Nov. 1962], p. 8). In an interview with Romero ("Panorama de arte y letras. Los barceloneses de *La noria* reaparecen en *La corriente*," *Destion* [June 30, 1962], p. 48) an unidentified critic does mention *The Others* as part of a three-novel "Human Comedy" along with *The Treadmill* and *The Current*, but fails to mention any elements that the first novel shares with the other two.

8. See "Panorama de . . . Los Barceloneses de. . . ," p. 48.

9. Romero also refers to characters of his first novel without treating

them specifically in *The Current*, as in the case of Mosén Bruguera, Doctor Luis Camps, and Doña Clara Seré. In a similar fashion, in the latter novel the author dedicates chapters to characters who were only mentioned in *The Treadmill* (Santiago, Raquel's husband, and "Trini's" daughter Vicentita, for example).

10. These characters, who appear frequently in *The Others*, receive only brief mention in *The Current*.

11. For example, Felipe and his bar appear in those chapters entitled "El Bar" and "Titirimundi"; Berta and her family appear in "La Familia," "Berta, La Buena," and "Almas y Cuerpos." Generally speaking, the titles of the chapters convey the essence of what they contain.

12. For examples, see pp. 7 and 49.

13. Quoted from an interview with Luis Romero ("Leer es lo que importa. Autores del día del libro," *Destino* [May 12, 1962], p. 41). See as well Romero's comments in another interview, "Panorama de arte y letras. Los barceloneses de *La noria* reaparecen en *La corriente*," *Destino* (June 30, 1962), p. 48.

14. Some examples are found on pp. 24, 56, 59, 67, 78, 92, 104–106, 115, 272.

15. Another example of this double perspective is seen in the case of Juanchu and Dorita (see pp. 170, 235).

Chapter Six

1. All references to *Shadows from Beyond* are based on the first edition (Madrid: Ediciones Cid, 1957).

2. "The Two Beggars" recalls another story by Luis Romero, "El niño enfermo" ("The Sick Boy") in *Asociación de la Parálisis Cerebral* (1961). In both stories, man finds consolation for his suffering in another individual who experiences deprivation and yet is capable of great compassion for humanity.

3. From a technical viewpoint, this remoteness is achieved by the use of the third-person perspective in describing autobiographical events. Thus, the story depends heavily on indirect interior monologue.

4. A third noticeable difference lies in the stories' means of expression. The third-person narrative prevails in "They Call This Judgment . . ." while in the other, the first person is used. The utilization of first person is appropriate for "This Strange White Wall" because here we witness the private disorientation of an individual. The third-person perspective as used in the other story is also artistically effective, for it strengthens the idea of evaluation of one's existence by outside entities.

5. Other examples of the absurd appear on pp. 109, 111–12. An excellent example is found on pp. 114–15, when an attorney "defends" the accused in a very unusual fashion (the worst part of all this is that everyone in the story perceives this absurd defense as effective). Needless to say, as the accused is confronted with so many meaningless arguments he becomes confused and

questions his own innocence (p. 112). Therefore, although for different reasons, man appears in both "They Call This Judgment. . ." and "This Strange White Wall" as unsure of himself.

6. A version of this story was published separately in 1953 (Madrid: Editorial Tecnos, "La Novela del Sábado"). No discernible differences have been detected between the two editions of this work.

7. Other examples can be found on pp. 178, 195, 200, 223.

8. All references to *Tudá* are based on the first edition (Barcelona: Ediciones Acervo, 1957).

9. The unity we are referring to is mentioned by Joaquín de Entrambasaguas, *Las mejores novelas contemporáneas*, Vol. 12 (Barcelona, Editorial Planeta, 1971), p. 1010. However, we do not go as far as this critic, who says that *Tudá* is a novel. In our opinion it remains a collection of short stories. Romero shares our view as documented in a letter to us dated February 7, 1975.

10. It is possible that *"There"* could refer to man's normal reaction toward wars: they always seem distant as long as we do not participate in them.

11. It should be noted that the characters do not always visualize their conflict at the Russian front as lacking in importance; often they consider themselves participants in a crusade against international Communism and for the preservation of Western civilization.

12. Madrid: Ediciones Cid, 1960. All references are to this edition.

13. Reference to the symbolism of the novel is made by Juan Luis Alborg, *Hora actual de la novela española*, Vol. 2 (Madrid: Taurus, 1962), p. 328.

14. Similar examples are found on pp. 153 and 228.

15. The theme of exploitation of the masses by the rich (or those who seek wealth) is another of the constants of Romero's work. The expression of this sincere preoccupation on the part of the novelist is weakened, however, by the overuse of the omniscient narrator to "tell" the reader what would be more effectively "discovered."

16. See examples on pp. 138–42 and 172–75. Social criticism as a theme of the novel has been discussed by Antonio Iglesias Laguna, *Treinta años de novela española (1938–1968)*, Vol. 1 (Madrid: Editorial Prensa Española, (1969), p. 299; Juan Ignacio Ferreras, *Tendencias de la novela española actual (1931–1969)* (Paris: Ediciones Hispanoamericanas, 1970), p. 157; and Joaquín de Entrambasaguas, *Las mejores novelas contemporáneas*, Vol. 12 (Barcelona: Editorial Planeta, 1971), p. 1012.

17. In the final pages of the novel, when describing the city in terms of its indifference to the birth of the child, the narrator abandons objectivity by using the first-person plural (p. 269). Although this is the only direct involvement by the narrator in the description of society, the tone of the narrative is often personal.

18. The following is a list of the narrative passages included in "The Treadmill of Memories": "Los arrabales" (June 15, 1963), "Noche de San Juan" (June 22, 1963), "Ugijar" (July 6, 1963), "Torremolinos" (July 27, 1963),

"El puerto de Vigo" (August 10, 1963), "Altamira" (August 24, 1963), "¡Culip, Culip!" (August 31, 1963), "Los grandes hombres" (September 7, 1963), "La dedicatoria" (September 21, 1963), "El puente del diablo" (October 5, 1963), "Sardinas" (October 26, 1963), "La Chanca" (November 2, 1963), "Los monederos falsos" (November 16, 1963), "Comida en el molino" (December 7, 1963), "San Juan de la Peña" (December 14, 1963), "La picota" (December 21, 1963), "Retorno a Bilbao" (January 11, 1964), "Año nuevo en Perguisa" (February 8, 1964), "Cádiz, desde un catalejo" (February 22, 1964), "La galerna" (March 7, 1964), "El leve recuerdo" (March 14, 1964), "Un vaso de buen vino" (March 28, 1964), "La mascletá" (April 11, 1964), "Saint Tropez" (May 9, 1964), "El entierro del niño" (May 16, 1964), "El mal recuerdo" (June 13, 1964), and "La bella desconocida" (July 11, 1964). Useful in locating these vignettes was the list of titles included by Entrambasaguas in his introduction to Luis Romero's works (p. 1020). Romero himself added eight titles to Entrambasaguas's catalogue in a letter to us dated May 21, 1975. We have not been able to locate two titles: "Molinos de Cartagena" (mentioned by Entrambasaguas) and "El mundo armónico" (mentioned by Romero in his letter). Perhaps there are others Romero himself has forgotten, for, as he has indicated, "a quarter of a century of work is too much, it extends and overflows . . ." (in a letter to us dated March 1, 1975).

19. An exception appears in "Un vaso de buen vino."

20. In a letter dated February 7, 1975, Romero indicates that most of his short stories except those published in *Shadows from Beyond* and *Tudá* are located in old journals that as a rule had brief life spans. Romero admits that these stories will be difficult to locate: he himself does not remember their whereabouts.

21. *Revista Ondas* (May 1, 1958).

22. *Miscellanea Barcinonensia. Revista de Investigación y Alta Cultura*, 2, No. 5 (1963), pp. 151–55.

23. *Q. P.*, No. 47 (February, 1971), pp. 9–13.

24. *Revista de Occidente*, No. 34 (January 1966), pp. 74–88.

25. *Revista de Occidente*, No. 111 (January 1972), pp. 320–34.

Chapter Seven

1. *El Cacique* (Barcelona: Editorial Planeta, 1963). All references and quotations are from the eighth printing ("edición") of 1967. In accordance with the rules of competition for the Planeta Prize, the novel was submitted by Romero under a pseudonym, "Fabián Suárez." There were 234 contestants. For further information about the selection of the prize-winning novel, see Fernando Vázquez-Prada, "Luis Romero, Premio Planeta con su obra 'El relevo,' " *Arriba* (October 14, 1963), p. 19. The original title of the novel, "The Changing of the Guard," suggests the succession of one *cacique* by another, something which is not implied by the title of the published work.

2. The idea that the *cacique* is the protagonist is generally accepted by critics of the novel, but some maintain that the real protagonist is the town, a contemporary and somewhat pathetic Fuenteovejuna. Among those who express the latter view are Antonio Iglesias Laguna, in *Treinta años de la novela española (1938–1968)*, Vol. 1 (Madrid: Editorial Prensa Española, 1969), p. 300; and Emiliano Aguado, (in his review of *El cacique*, in *La Estafeta Literaria*, No. 286 (1964), p. 20. The view that the *cacique* is the protagonist is held by such critics as Joaquín de Entrambasaguas (*Las mejores novelas contemporáneas*, Vol. 12 [Barcelona: Editorial Planeta, 1971], p. 1015); Albert Mazzetti (Review of *El cacique*, in *Reseña de la Literatura, Arte y Espectáculos*, No. 1 [1964]); and Paulino Posada (Review of *El cacique*, in *Indice de Arte y Letras*, No. 182 [March 1964], p. 27).

3. In a way, the successful action of the circus performers contrasts with the ineptness of the townspeople and is an implicit insult to their weakness.

4. On the subject of ambiguity in literature, we refer the reader to William Empson's *Seven Types of Ambiguity*, 3rd ed. (Norfolk: New Directions Books, 1953); P. M. Wetherill's *The Literary Text: An Examination of Critical Methods* (Berkeley and Los Angeles: University of California Press, 1974); and Ernesto Sábato's *El escritor y sus fantasmas, Obras. Ensayos* (Buenos Aires: Editorial Losada, 1970).

5. *Figures*, Vol. I (Paris: Editions Du Sevil, 1966), p. 203.

6. Carlos Luis Alvarez ("*El Cacique*, por Luis Romero," *Blanco y Negro*, No. 2695 [December 28, 1963] suggests that the rapid change of scenes which are often unrelated in time and place contributes as well to a sensation of simultaneity on the part of the reader.

7. This is not to say, of course, that interior monologue and description by the omniscient narrator are completely lacking, but that their relative frequency is greatly reduced.

8. Paulino Posada finds the use of dialogue tiresome, and laments the predominance of this technique at the expense of descriptive passages. Most commentators, however, agree that Romero's dialogues are crisp and lively. The particular merit of this means of expression is the successful use of colloquial speech patterns and vocabulary. Posada himself recognizes this quality.

9. *Valle-Inclán: Anatomía de un teatro problemático* (Madrid: Editorial Fundamentos, 1972), p. 22.

10. Antonio Iglesias Laguna (p. 300) has mentioned briefly the presence of the static in *The Cacique*.

11. Rodolfo Cardona and Anthony N. Zahareas, *Visión del esperpento. Teoría y práctica en los esperpentos de Valle-Inclán* (Madrid: Editorial Castalia, 1970), p. 11.

12. Ibid., pp. 30–32.

13. In Valle-Inclán's *Bohemian Lights*, trans. by Anthony N. Zahareas and Gerald Gillespie (Austin: University of Texas Press, 1976), Max Estrella ellaborates on the function of distortions in modern Spanish art:

MAX: Don Latino de Hispalis, grotesque figure, I shall make you immortal in a novel!
DON LATINO: In a tragedy, Max.
MAX: Our tragedy is no longer a tragedy.
DON LATINO: But it's got to be something!
MAX: *Esperpento*.
DON LATINO: Don't twist your mouth, Max.
MAX: I'm freezing to death!
DON LATINO: Come on, get up. Let's start walking.
MAX: I can't, I tell you.
DON LATINO: Stop this farce. Let's take a walk.
MAX: Breathe hard on me. Where have you gone, Latino?
DON LATINO: I'm at your side.
MAX: Since you've been transformed into an Ox, I can't recognize you. Breathe on me, Illustrious Ox from Bethlehem's stable. Bellow, Latino! You are the bell-ox, and if you bellow hard, the Sacred Bull will appear. We'll play torero with him.
DON LATINO: You're beginning to frighten me. You should drop that joke.
MAX: The avant-garde are humbugs. It was Goya who invented the Grotesque. The classical heroes have gone to take a stroll in Cat Alley.
DON LATINO: You're completely balmy.
MAX: Classical heroes reflected in concave mirrors yield the Grotesque. The tragic sense of Spanish life can be rendered only through an aesthetic that is systematically deformed.
DON LATINO: Catshit! You're about to catch that disease yourself!
MAX: Spain is a grotesque deformation of European civilization.
DON LATINO: Perhaps! I'm staying out of all this!
MAX: In a concave mirror, even the most beautiful images are absurd.
DON LATINO: Agreed. But I enjoy looking at myself in the mirrors in Cat Alley.
MAX: Me too. Deformation stops being deformation when subjected to a perfect mathematic. My present aesthetic approach is to transform all classical norms with the mathematics of the concave mirror. (p. 183)

14. By "a better novel" we mean one more like Valle-Inclán's *Tirano Banderas*.

15. Pablo Gil Casado, *La novela social española (1942–1968)* (Barcelona: Editorial Seix Barral, S.A., 1968), pp. 122–23, has mentioned briefly the existence of similarities between *El Cacique* and the *esperpento*. In doing this, Gil Casado was referring to the character Colibrí and his way of speaking.

16. It is surprising that in the opinion of José R. Marra-López (review of *El Cacique, Insula*, 208 [March 1964], p. 9), this novel has nothing new to offer.

Chapter Eight

1. Among others, José Luis S. Ponce de León, *La novela española de la Guerra Civil (1936–1939)* (Madrid: Insula, 1971), p. 105; José Luis Cano, "Los libros del mes. Luis Romero: *Tres días de julio*," *Insula*, 247 (June 1967), pp. 8–9; Emiliano Aguado, "Las gafas sin cristal. La prosa. España sufrida, sufrida España. Tres días apocalípticos," *La Estafeta Literaria*, 370

(1967), p. 25; Salvador Corberó, "El alzamiento de Cartagena reconstruido por Luis Romero," *Diario de Barcelona* (June 13, 1971); José Corrales Egea, *La novela española actual* (Madrid: Editorial Cuadernos para el Diálogo, 1971), pp. 164–65. Although he refers to the historical nature of the book, Corrales Egea prefers to call *Three Days in July* a novel.

2. "Prologue" to *Three Days in July*, p. xxxix. All references to this work are based on the third edition (Barcelona: Ediciones Ariel, 1972).

3. *Discuros leídos ante la Real Academia Española en las recepciones públicas del 7 y 21 de febrero de 1897* (Madrid: Est. Tip. de la Viuda e Hijos de Tello, 1897), pp. 11–12. Amado Alonso *(Ensayo sobre la novela histórica* [Buenos Aires: Facultad de Filosofía y Letras de la Universidad de Buenos Aires, 1942], pp. 9–145) has discussed many of the problems confronted in the writing of an historical novel (for instance, the creative stagnation of the writer as he attempts to make his work conform to history).

4. *Three Days in July*, p. xxxix.

5. Diana Spearman, *The Novel and Society* (New York: Barnes & Noble, Inc., 1966), p. 147, is speaking of the novel in general in this passage.

6. Spearman, p. 148, has referred to how "the picture of any society given in its literature does not always agree with the picture given by historians." History—the Spanish Civil War—as used by a novelist is the topic of an interesting essay written by Paul Ilie ("Fictive History in Gironella," *Journal of Spanish Studies: Twentieth Century*, 2 [1974], pp. 77–94).

7. This statement appears on the book's jacket (Barcelona-Caracas-Mexico: Editorial Ariel, 1976).

8. Spearman, p. 150, is referring to those obstacles the novelist faces in trying to record life. In the "Prologue" of *Disaster in Cartagena* (Barcelona: Editorial Ariel, 1971), pp. 9–11 and 36, Romero describes how he found it impossible to give a literary treatment to the information he had gathered on the end of the Civil War (this information later became *The End of the War*, a work of history). Therefore, he decided to write on a specific event which was suitable to a literary approach: the revolt at Cartagena. On the limitations of "realistic photography" by novelists, we refer the reader to N. Elizabeth Monroe, *The Novel and Society* (Port Washington, New York: Kennikat Press, Inc., 1965), pp. 15–16.

9. Aguado, p. 25.

10. Much of what happens in *Three Days in July* is ironic. It is through this irony that the reader's perception of the cruelty of war is intensified. One example should suffice to demonstrate our position. On page 503 a soldier is hit by sniper fire, and his fellow soldiers realize that they must silence this hidden enemy or all of them could suffer the same fate as their comrade. The irony lies in the reaction of the corporal in charge to what has taken place: "The rest [come] with me, we are going to cross over there. We are going to hunt that son of a bitch . . ." (p. 504). In his comments, the corporal insults the enemy for having the same motivations as do he and those with him

(namely, to kill). This example illustrates some of the basic elements of irony as studied by D. C. Muecke, *The Compass of Irony* (London: Methuen & Co., Ltd., 1969) and Wayne C. Booth, *A Rhetoric of irony* (Chicago and London: the University of Chicago Press, 1974); the corporal's reaction is an example of *literary* irony (and not merely situational irony) because the author has a deliberate intention in placing this particular corporal, an incarnation of conflicting attitudes, within his work. With the corporal's insult, we can perceive that irony "is the art of saying something without really saying it. It is an art that gets its effects from below the surface . . ." (Muecke, p. 5).

11. Among the characters appears Francisco Gallardo, whom we had already met in *The Treadmill* ("Historia proletaria," pp. 46–51). In both works, his traits are identical (for a comparison see pp. 47–48 of *The Treadmill* and pp. 35, 386–88 of *Three Days in July*). Is Francisco Gallardo a fictional character in view of his existence elsewhere in Romero's production? Does he illustrate a weakening in Romero's desire to present historical facts? Could he have existed? In his "Onomastic Index" to *Three Days in July* Romero places an asterisk before Gallardo's name, indicating that his name was other than Gallardo or that this is a personage reconstructed from those individuals Romero knew during the Civil War (p. 627).

12. The pages are filled with references to characters (historical and fictional), events, and dates which are significant in analyzing the period in question. Note that the work has 617 pages of narrative, and an index of photographs, characters, and cities of twenty-one pages.

13. As Corrales Egea does (p. 165).

14. It is interesting that the role of General Franco, although important and revealing, does not dominate the pages of *Three Days in July*. Most of the emphasis is given to the reaction on the mainland to the bold action of the Spanish army in Africa. In doing this, Romero remains true to history, for during the first few days of the Civil War Franco did not have the importance he acquired by the end of this conflict. For one thing, there were too many prominent leaders still alive at the beginning of the war.

15. For Corrales Egea, however, the abundance of facts is not a weak point of the work (p. 164).

16. "I write a chronicle of three decisive days, not a sparkling literary work. I speak, I write, simply and directly, the only way to approach the theme" (p. xxix). His prologue is not only an explanation of procedures used to collect the historical data for the book, but also a defense of his work as a chronicle of certain literary dimensions.

17. Monroe's comments on the failure of the "proletarian novelists" is revealing (p. 16). Also of interest is the following statement by Robert Scholes (*Structuralism in Literature* [New Haven: Yale University Press, 1974], p. 132): "Fiction can give us the degraded world of satire, the heroic world of romance or the mimetic world of history."

18. For a few of the many examples of this lack of precision concerning point of view, see pp. 3, 151–52, 229, 308.

19. In his "prologue," Romero insists that his primary motivation in writing *Three Days in July* was to argue that never again should Spaniards allow themselves to enter into such a war, a lesson of history that must be imprinted forever in the minds and hearts of his countrymen (p. xxxvi).

20. *Desastre en Cartagena* (*marzo de 1939*). Barcelona: Ediciones Ariel, 1971. All references to this work are based on this edition. This work, like *Three Days in July,* is followed by an "Onomastic Index" (pp. 305–309). However, in *Disaster in Cartagena*'s index very few names are preceded by an asterisk, a fact which tells us that in his second book on the Civil War Romero has reconstructed few characters and has made less use of his abilities as a novelist (see note 11).

21. In the "Prologue" Romero states, "I have chosen the literary style in which the book is written in order to be able to take [certain] liberties and to [facilitate] the better understanding of the characters, circumstances, motives and dilemmas and the actions themselves. But I have not followed this rule rigidly; *Disaster in Cartagena* is not a literary exercise, rather I consider it a history book with the purpose of transmitting to others that which in one way or another I have been able to uncover" (p. 36).

22. Although the action occurs primarily in Cartagena, there is a brief scene at Franco's headquarters in Burgos and considerable communication by telegraph between Cartagena and Burgos.

23. In another example, the "sentence" is reduced to a series of nouns: "It becomes difficult to determine who the rebels are and who are the prisoners. [People] running, voices, insults, shouts of 'viva,' threats. New doors which face the outside are opened; no one knows who has done it. More soldiers who enter. Shortly the attackers control the main floor" (p. 254).

24. All references to *The End of the War* are taken from the edition published in Barcelona-Caracas-Mexico by Editorial Ariel in 1976.

25. It should be noted that we are not addressing ourselves to the historical merit of *The End of the War* even though it is this aspect of the work which according to Luis Romero determines the value of the book. We chose to approach *The End of the War* from a literary perspective because of the many traits it shares with *Three Days in July* and *Disaster in Cartagena.*

26. Malcolm Alan Compitello, in his review of Luis and Antolín González-del-Valle's *La ficción de Luis Romero* (*The American Hispanist,* 1, No. 9 [May 1976], p. 15) holds a different view concerning the thematic and artistic value of *Three Days in July* in particular. Perhaps Professor Compitello's position results from an excessive dependence on certain critics (Corrales Egea, Ferreras, Ponce) who have in a few sentences considered the merits of *Three Days in July.* It should be noted that we do not object to Romero's use of history. To us the problem is one of how he uses it, or how he allows it to hinder his "novelistic talents."

Chapter Nine

1. Rafael Delgado, "El arte y sus intérpretes. Una charla de Café con el Premio Nadal 1951, Luis Romero, novelista." *Índice Literario*, Supplement of *El Universal* (May 20, 1958), p. 4.

Selected Bibliography

PRIMARY SOURCES

Works by Luis Romero in chronological order and by genres.

1. Novels

La noria. Barcelona: Ediciones Destino, 1952.
Carta de ayer. Barcelona: Editorial Planeta, 1953.
Las viejas voces. Barcelona: Editorial Exito, S.A., 1955.
Los otros. Barcelona: Ediciones Destino, 1956.
La finestra, J. J. Goldemberg. "Camallarg" i la ciencia nuclear. Barcelona: Albertí Editor, 1956 (the last two titles are short stories, all three in Catalan).
El carrer. Barcelona: Albertí Editor. 1959 (in Catalan).
La noche buena. Madrid: Ediciones Cid. 1960.
La corriente. Barcelona: Ediciones Destino, 1962.
El cacique. Barcelona: Editorial Planeta, 1963.

2. Short Stories

Ha pasado una sombra. Madrid: Editorial Tecnos, "La Novela del Sábado," 1953. This story appeared later in *Shadows from Beyond.*
Esas sombras del trasmundo. Madrid: Ediciones Cid, 1957 (a collection of stories).
Tudá. Barcelona: Ediciones Acervo, 1957 (a collection of stories).
"La barca." *Revista Ondas* (May 1, 1958).
"El niño enfermo." *Asociación de la Parálisis Cerebral (December 1961).*
"El cumpleaños de Elena." *Miscellanea Barcinonensia. Revista de Investigación y Alta Cultura,* 2, No. 5 (1963), pp. 151–55.
"El hombre justo." *Revista de Occidente,* 34 (January 1966), 74–88.
"La Playa." *Q. P.,* 47 (February 1971), 10–12.
"El día en que terminó la guerra." *Revista de Occidente,* 111 (June 1972), 320–34.

3. Historical Works

Tres días de julio. Barcelona: Ediciones Ariel, 1967.
Desastre en Cartagena. Marzo de 1939. Barcelona: Editorial Ariel, 1971.
El final de la guerra. Barcelona-Caracas-Mexico: Editorial Ariel, 1976.

131

4. Other Creative Works
Cuerda tensa. Barcelona, 1950. Poetry.
"La noria de los recuerdos." *Destino.* In 1963: June 15 and 22, July 6 and 27,
   August 10, 24, and 31, September 7 and 21, October 5 and 26,
   November 2 and 16, December 7, 14, and 21; and 1964: January 11,
   February 8 and 22, March 7, 14, and 28, April 11, May 9 and 16, June 13,
   July 11.
For the individual titles of the realistic vignettes of "La noria de los
   recuerdos," see chapter 6, note 18.

5. Travel Books
Tabernas. Barcelona–Buenos Aires: Librería Editorial Argos, S.A., 1950.
Barcelona. Illustrations by Francisco Catalá Roca. Barcelona: Editorial
   Barna, S.A., 1954.
Libro de las tabernas de España. Barcelona: Editorial AHR, 1956.
Costa Brava. Photographs by F. Catalá Roca. Madrid: Ediciones Cid, 1958.

6. Essays and Lectures
"Boris Pasternak." *Diario de Barcelona* (December 7, 1958).
"En busca de los primitivos barceloneses." *Destino* (January 2, 1960), 13–15.
"El dedo en la llaga." *Diario de Barcelona* (January 18, 1961), 5.
"Hemingway estaba envejeciendo." *Diario de Barcelona* (July 21, 1961).
"Introducción." *Tharrats.* Santander: Publicaciones La Isla de los Ratones,
   1961, 9–24.
"La gran crisis." *Diario de Barcelona* (March 22, 1962).
"Perfiles humanos de la actividad aseguradora." Lecture delivered on June
   1963 at the end of academic year 1962–1963 of the Escuela Profesional
   del Sindicato del Seguro, 7–22.
"Cuando el agua se vuelve solanesca." *Agua* (July-August 1963), 2–5.
"Otra visita al Prado. Historias de la historia." *La Vanguardia Española*
   (January 22, 1965).
"III. España moderna." "IV. España en fiestas." *Sobre la piel de toro.*
   Barcelona: Aymá, 1965. Chapters from a book.
"El libro, el autor y el editor." Lecture delivered at the Biblioteca Central de
   Barcelona. April 24, 1967, 53–61.
"Picasso en Cataluña, I–III." *La Vanguardia Española* (June 7, 13, and 20,
   1967).
"Colaboración de la vanguardia. Despedida. Marcel Duchamp."
   La Vanguardia Española (October 5, 1968), p. 12.
"Ecos de la vida literaria. Las lecturas. Llordes, el soldado."
   La Vanguardia Española (January 2, 1969).
"Viaje a Checoslovaquia, I–VIII." *La Vanguardia Española* (June 28 and July
   1, 2, 4, 8, 9, 11, and 15, 1969).
"El autor y su obra." *La noria.* Barcelona: Círculo de Lectores, 1971. No
   pagination. Autobiographical preface to this edition of *The Treadmill.*

"Donde nacen los ríos, I–IV." *La Vanguardia Española* (December 8, 13, and 22, 1972, and January 5, 1973).

"Exposiciones en Cadaqués, I." *La Vanguardia Española* (August 28, 1973).

"Presencia." *Papeles de Son Armadans*, 215 (February 1974), 193–96.

"Las batallas perdidas. Incongruencia." *La Vanguardia Española* (May 22, 1974).

"De Hamilton a Goldini. Crónica del recuento." *La Vanguardia Española* (September 27, 1974).

7. Interviews
   The interviewer's name is provided at the start of each entry.

Arce, Manuel. "En una taberna con Luis Romero." *Indice de artes y letras*, 52 (June 15, 1952), 6.

Cano, José Luis. "Charlas en Insula. Luis Romero." *Insula*, 110 (February 15, 1955), 8.

Manzano, Rafael. "Luis Romero opina que el escritor, en España, puede vivir de la literatura." *La Estafeta Literaria*, 79 (January 19, 1957).

Delgado, Rafael. "El arte y sus intérpretes. Una charla de café con el Premio Nadal 1951, Luis Romero, novelista." *Indice Literario*, supplement of *El Universal* (May 20, 1958), 4. Borras Betriu, Rafael. "Galería de retratos. Luis Romero."
La Jirafa, (1958), 8–9.

Bonet, Laurentino. "Entrevista con Luis Romero." *Destino*, 1347 (June 1, 1963), 45.

Olmos García, Francisco. "La novela y los novelistas españoles de hoy." *Cuadernos Americanos*, 129 (July-August 1963), 211–37.

Trenas, Julio. "Luis Romero afirma: 'Los novelistas actuales y la vida española se han influido mutuamente.' " *Pueblo* (December 11, 1963), 24.

"Luis Permanyer presenta a: Luis Romero (a través del cuestionario 'Marcel Proust')." *Destino*, 1378 (January 3, 1964), 37.

Mostaza, Bartolomé. "Luis Romero: Su obra y su actitud." *El libro español*, 7 (February 1964), 45–48.

Soldevila-Durante, Ignacio. "Entrevista a Luis Romero." Transcription by José Varela Muñoz. Unpublished document. March 13, 1965.

"El escritor y su espejo. Luis Romero." *ABC* (September 15, 1965).

Paniker, Salvador. "Luis Romero." *Conversaciones en Cataluña*. Barcelona: Editorial Kairos, 1966.

Heras, Antonio R. de las. "Escritores al habla. Luis Romero." *ABC* (March 27, 1969).

Gironella, José Luis. "Luis Romero novelista." *100 Españoles y Dios*. Barcelona: Ediciones Nauta, 1969.

Illa Morell, Juan. "Luis Romero." *Revista Vallés* (February 21, 1970).

Fernández-Braso, Miguel. "Luis Romero: prisionero literario de la Guerra Civil." *De escritor a escritor*. Barcelona: Editorial Taber, 1970.

Sabater, Enrique. "Diálogos en la Costa Brava. Luis Romero, un escritor enamorado de Cadaqués." *Diario de Gerona* (July 16, 1971), 5.

————. "Diálogos en la Costa Crava. Luis Romero prepara un nuevo libro sobre la etapa final de nuestra guerra." *Diario de Gerona* (July 17, 1971) 6.

González-del-Valle, Luis and Antolín González-del-Valle. "Entrevista a Luis Romero." Unpublished document. October 1973.

Clemente, J. C. "A tumba abierta. Luis Romero, entre la novela y la historia." *Diario de Barcelona* (November 18, 1973).

Carol, José. "Luis Romero. Novelista, historiador de la Guerra Civil." *Entre la espada y la pared.* Barcelona: Ediciones Sertebi, 1974.

González-del-Valle, Luis and Antolín. "Entrevista a Luis Romero." *Hispania*, 58 (March 1975), 215–16.

SECONDARY SOURCES

The bibliography of Romero's literary production is quite limited. Most existing critical evaluations are reviews or brief commentaries in histories of the novel.

ALBORG, JUAN LUIS. "Luis Romero." *Hora actual de la novela española.* Vol. 2. Madrid: Taurus, 1962, 311–31. One of the few extensive studies on Romero, now outdated. It contains serious misinterpretations. For instance, *Christmas Eve* is viewed as a highly poetic work when, in fact, it is a simplistic novel.

CASTELLET, JOSÉ MARÍA. "*La noria.*" *Notas sobre literatura española contemporánea.* Barcelona: Ediciones Laye, 1955, 55–57. This brief evaluation of *The Treadmill* misunderstands fundamental aspects of the novel.

ENTRAMBASAGUAS, JOAQUÍN DE. "Luis Romero." *Las mejores novelas contemporáneas.* Vol 12, Barcelona: Editorial Planeta, 1971, 995–1024. An overview of Romero's life and work that fails to go beyond the most obvious aspects of Romero's literary production. Parts of the study were published as book reviews. A bibliography consisting mainly of reviews and brief evaluations accompanies the essay.

GIL CASADO, PABLO, *La novela social española (1942–1968).* Barcelona: Editorial Seix Barral, S.A., 1968 121–23, 263–64, 265–69. Some works by Romero are considered as Gil Casado examines the different characteristics of the social novel.

GONZÁLEZ-DEL-VALLE, LUIS and ANTOLÍN. *La ficción de Luis Romero. Estudio monográfico.* Manhattan: Society of Spanish and Spanish-American Studies, 1976. A reproduction of an essay published in *Cuadernos Hispanoamericanos*, 302 (August 1975), 346–400. This is the first lengthy study on Romero. It fails to consider many of his works and his life.

GRUPP, WILLIAM JOHN. "Two Novels by Luis Romero." *Hispania*, 39 (1956), 201–205. The first serious attempt at understanding *The Treadmill* and *Letter from the Past.*

IGLESIAS LAGUNA, ANTONIO. *Treinta años de novela española.* Vol. 1. Madrid: Editorial "Prensa Española," 1969, 297–301. An overview of Romero's works.

NORA, EUGENIO DE. *La novela española contemporánea (1939–1967).* 2nd edition. Vol. 3. Madrid: Editorial Gredos. S.A., 1970, 150–52. A panoramic commentary.

Index